First World War
and Army of Occupation
War Diary
France, Belgium and Germany

14 DIVISION
Divisional Troops
Royal Army Veterinary Corps
26 Mobile Veterinary Section
21 May 1915 - 26 February 1919

WO95/1892/4

The Naval & Military Press Ltd
www.nmarchive.com
Published in association with The National Archives

Published by

The Naval & Military Press Ltd

Unit 10 Ridgewood Industrial Park,

Uckfield, East Sussex,

TN22 5QE England

Tel: +44 (0) 1825 749494

www.naval-military-press.com

www.nmarchive.com

This diary has been reprinted in facsimile from the original. Any imperfections are inevitably reproduced and the quality may fall short of modern type and cartographic standards.

© **Crown Copyright**
Images reproduced by permission of The National Archives, London, England, 2015.

Contents

Document type	Place/Title	Date From	Date To
Heading	1892/4		
Heading	14th Division 26th Mobile Vety Section May 1915-Feb 1919		
Heading	14th Division 26th Mobile Vet Section Vol. I 21.5-30.6.15 To Feb 19		
War Diary		21/05/1915	30/06/1915
Heading	14th Division 26th Mobile Vety Section Vol II 1-3 1-7-15		
War Diary	In The Field	01/07/1915	31/07/1915
Heading	14th Division 26th Mobile Vet Section Vol III August 15		
War Diary	In The Field	25/08/1915	31/08/1915
War Diary	In The Field	01/08/1915	24/08/1915
Heading	14th Division 26th Mobile Vet. Section Vol. IV. Sept 15		
War Diary	In The Field	01/09/1915	30/09/1915
Heading	14th Division 26th Mob. Vet. Sect. Vol. 5 Oct 15		
War Diary	Watou	01/10/1915	31/10/1915
Heading	14th Division Nov. 15 26th Mobs. Vet. Sect. Vol: 6		
War Diary	Watou	01/11/1915	30/11/1915
Heading	14th Division 26th Mob: Veb. Feel Vol: 7		
War Diary	Watou	01/12/1915	31/01/1916
Heading	14 26th Mob Vet. Sect Vol. 9		
War Diary	Watou.	02/02/1916	14/02/1916
War Diary	Ledringhem	15/02/1916	19/02/1916
War Diary	Watou	20/02/1916	22/02/1916
War Diary	St. Vaast En Chausse	23/02/1916	24/02/1916
War Diary	Beauval	25/02/1916	25/02/1916
War Diary	Doullens	26/02/1916	26/02/1916
War Diary	Etree Wamin	27/02/1916	28/02/1916
War Diary	Blavincourt	29/02/1916	01/03/1916
War Diary	Barly	02/03/1916	18/03/1916
War Diary	Fosseux	19/03/1916	31/03/1916
Heading	26 M Vet's Vol 10		
War Diary	Fosseux	01/04/1916	04/04/1916
War Diary	Filescamp	05/05/1916	31/05/1916
War Diary	Filescamp Farm	01/06/1916	29/07/1916
War Diary	Sus St Leger	30/07/1916	30/07/1916
War Diary	Frohen Le Grand	31/07/1916	31/07/1916
Heading	War Diary. Of 26th Vet, Mobile Section. August 1916 (Volume)		
War Diary	Frohen Le Grand	01/08/1916	01/08/1916
War Diary	Bernaville	02/08/1916	07/08/1916
War Diary	Albert	08/08/1916	13/08/1916
War Diary	Ribemont	14/08/1916	31/08/1916
War Diary	St Saveur	01/09/1916	01/09/1916
War Diary	Boisrault	02/09/1916	03/09/1916
War Diary	Ferme St Larme	04/09/1916	10/09/1916
War Diary	Ailly Sur Somme	11/09/1916	11/09/1916
War Diary	Buire	12/09/1916	12/09/1916

War Diary	Albert	13/09/1916	17/09/1916
War Diary	Buire	18/09/1916	21/09/1916
War Diary	Talmas	22/09/1916	22/09/1916
War Diary	Brevillers	23/09/1916	27/09/1916
War Diary	Fosseux	28/09/1916	30/09/1916
Heading	War Diary Of 26th Mobile Veterinary Section. October 1st 1916 To October 31st 1916		
War Diary	Fosseux	01/10/1916	27/10/1916
War Diary	Lattre St Quentin	28/10/1916	31/10/1916
Heading	War Diary Of Capt War A.V.C. O.C 26 Mob. Vety Location From 1st Nov. 1916 To 30 Nov. 1916 Volume 18		
War Diary	Lattre St. Quentin	01/11/1916	08/11/1916
War Diary	Farm Mount Joie	08/11/1916	30/11/1916
Heading	War Diary Of O.C. 26th Mobile Veterinary Section From 1st December 1916 To 31st December 1916 (Volume No. 19)		
War Diary	Farm Mont-La-Joie	01/12/1916	19/12/1916
War Diary	Fosseux	20/12/1916	31/12/1916
Heading	War Diary Of O.C. 26th M V S. From 1st Jany 1917 (Volume No 44)		
War Diary	Fosseux	01/01/1917	31/01/1917
Heading	War Diary Of O.C. 26th M.V.S. From 1st February To 28th February 17		
War Diary	Fosseux	01/02/1917	28/02/1917
Heading	War Diary Of O.C. 26th M.V.S. Volume 46 (Mar 1st To Mar 31st 1917)		
War Diary	Fosseux	01/03/1917	31/03/1917
Heading	War Diary Of O.C. 26th M.V.S. April 1st To April 30th 17 (Volume 47)		
Heading	Confidential		
War Diary	Fosseux	01/04/1917	02/04/1917
War Diary	Simencourt	03/04/1917	15/04/1917
War Diary	Le Cauroy	16/04/1917	23/04/1917
War Diary	Fosseux	24/04/1917	24/04/1917
War Diary	Bellacourt	25/04/1917	26/04/1917
War Diary	Berneville	27/04/1917	30/04/1917
Heading	War Diary Of O.C. 26th M. V. S. From May 1st To May 31st 1917 (Volume 48)		
Heading	War Diary Of O.C. 26th M.V.S.		
War Diary	Berneville	01/05/1917	15/05/1917
War Diary	Agny	16/05/1917	13/06/1917
War Diary	Monchiet	14/05/1917	14/05/1917
War Diary	Larbret	15/05/1917	15/05/1917
War Diary	St Leger Les Authie	16/05/1917	30/05/1917
Heading	War Diary Of O.C. 26th M. V. S. July 1st To July 31st 1917 (Volume 50)		
War Diary	St Leger Les Authie	01/07/1917	10/07/1917
War Diary	Gezaincourt	11/07/1917	11/07/1917
War Diary	St. Jans Cappel	12/07/1917	31/07/1917
Heading	War Diary Of O.C. 26th M. V. S. From Aug 1st To Aug. 31st 1917 (Volume No 51)		
War Diary	St Jans Cappel	01/08/1917	06/08/1917
War Diary	Pradelles	07/08/1917	15/08/1917
War Diary	Sheet 27 L 24 C.2.9	16/08/1917	31/08/1917

Heading	War Diary Of O.C. 26th M. V. S. September 1st To 30th 1917 (Volume No. 52)		
War Diary	Fletre	01/09/1917	04/09/1917
War Diary	Sheet 28	05/09/1917	05/09/1917
War Diary	Sheet 28 S 29.a.2.4	06/09/1917	30/09/1917
Heading	War Diary Of O.C. 26th M.V.S. From Oct 1st To Oct 31st 1917 (Volume No. 53)		
War Diary	Sheet 28 S 29.a.2.4	01/10/1917	09/10/1917
War Diary	M16.a.5.7	10/10/1917	11/10/1917
War Diary	Sheet 28 M 6.a.2.7	12/10/1917	24/10/1917
War Diary	Sheet 27 R4 a.7.2	24/10/1917	31/10/1917
Heading	War Diary Of O.C. 26th M.V.S. From Nov 1st To Nov 30th 1917 (Volume No. 54)		
War Diary	Sheet 27. R 4 a 7.2	01/11/1917	12/11/1917
War Diary	Wizernes	13/11/1917	30/11/1917
Heading	War Diary Of O.C. 26th M.V.S. Dec. 1st To Dec. 31st 1917 (Volume No 55)		
War Diary	Wizernes	01/12/1917	03/12/1917
War Diary	Sheet 28 G 11 a 5.6	04/12/1917	26/12/1917
War Diary	Wizernes	27/12/1917	31/12/1917
Heading	War Diary Of O.C. 26 M.V.S. January 1st To 31st (Volume No. 56)		
War Diary	Bray-Sur-Somme	09/01/1918	19/01/1918
War Diary	Wizernes	01/01/1918	04/01/1918
War Diary	Bray-Sur-Somme	04/01/1918	22/01/1918
War Diary	Rosieve en Sanlenis	23/01/1918	23/01/1918
War Diary	Davenscourt	24/01/1918	24/01/1918
War Diary	Candor	25/01/1918	25/01/1918
War Diary	Tirlancourt	26/01/1918	28/01/1918
War Diary	Fussy	29/01/1918	31/01/1918
Heading	War Diary Of O.C. 26th M.V.S. 14 Division February 1st To 28th (Volume No 57)		
War Diary	Fussy	01/02/1918	28/02/1918
Heading	War Diary Of O.C. 26 M.V.S. From April 1st To April 30th 1918 (Volume No)		
War Diary	Boursines	01/04/1918	01/04/1918
War Diary	Vers	02/04/1918	02/04/1918
War Diary	Sheet Amiens 17 D 2	03/04/1918	08/04/1918
War Diary	Fresnoy Au Val	08/04/1918	08/04/1918
War Diary	Frucourt	09/04/1918	09/04/1918
War Diary	Feuquieres	10/04/1918	11/04/1918
War Diary	Preures	12/04/1918	19/04/1918
War Diary	Cavron-St-Martin	20/04/1918	30/04/1918
Heading	War Diary Of O.C. 26th M.V.S. From 1st To 31st May 1918		
War Diary	Cavron-St-Martin	01/05/1918	02/05/1918
War Diary	Torcy	03/05/1918	09/06/1918
War Diary	Delette	10/06/1918	10/06/1918
War Diary	L'Oblois Wood N.17 a 7.3	11/06/1918	30/06/1918
War Diary	Oblois Wood	01/07/1918	11/07/1918
War Diary	Clerques	12/07/1918	12/07/1918
War Diary	Eperlecques	13/07/1918	31/07/1918
Miscellaneous	School Of Horn Matendship At Mobile Veg Section		
War Diary	Eperlecques.	01/08/1918	18/08/1918
War Diary	Bissezelle	19/08/1918	19/08/1918
War Diary	Stratcona Sheet 27 F13.D.1.9	20/08/1918	31/08/1918

Heading	War Diary Of O.C. 26th M.V.S. September 1st To 30th 1918 Vol 40		
War Diary	Stratcona Camp Sheet 27 F13 D1.9.	01/09/1918	19/09/1918
War Diary	Sheet 27 L23 4.9	20/09/1918	23/09/1918
War Diary	Breda Farm Sheet 27 L23 D 4.9	26/09/1918	30/09/1918
Heading	War Diary Of O.C. 26th M.V.S. 1st To 31st October 18		
War Diary	Breda Farm Sh.27. L23d 4.9	01/10/1918	02/10/1918
War Diary	Neuve Eglise Sh 28. T14 D 2.8	03/10/1918	18/10/1918
War Diary	Wervick Sud Hazebrouck Chateau	19/10/1918	20/10/1918
War Diary	Farme Montagne Sh 28.x29b-2.8 Turcoing	21/10/1918	31/10/1918
Heading	War Diary Of O.C. 26 M.V.S. 1st To 30th November 1918 Vol 43		
War Diary	Farme Montagne Sh. 28X29 B2.8 Turcoing	01/11/1918	03/11/1918
War Diary	Sh. 37. A 21 C 2.8 Watrelos	04/11/1918	30/11/1918
Heading	War Diary Of O.C. 26 M.V.S. (From 1st To 31st Dec. 1918)		
War Diary	Wattrelos Sheet 37 A 21. C 2.8.	01/12/1918	22/12/1918
War Diary	Sheet 37 A 27 A 5.7	23/12/1918	26/12/1918
War Diary	Roubaix Sheet 37 A 27 A 5 7	27/12/1918	31/12/1918
Heading	War Diary Of O.C. 26th M.V.S. (January 1st To 31st 1919)		
War Diary	Wattrelos Sheet 37 A 27 A 5 7	01/01/1919	31/01/1919
Heading	War Diary Of O.C. 26 M.V.S. (1st To 28th February 1919)		
War Diary	Rombai	01/02/1919	12/03/1919
War Diary	Tourcoing	12/02/1919	26/02/1919

1892/4

14TH DIVISION

26TH MOBILE VETY SECTION

MAY 1915 - FEB 1919

121/6111

avS

14th Division

26th Mobile Vety Section.

Vol. I. 21.5 — 30.6.15.

E

Dec '19

Army Form C. 2118.

WAR DIARY
or
INTELLIGENCE SUMMARY.

(Erase heading not required.)

Instructions regarding War Diaries and Intelligence Summaries are contained in F. S. Regs., Part II. and the Staff Manual respectively. Title pages will be prepared in manuscript.

Place	Date	Hour	Summary of Events and Information	Remarks and references to Appendices.
	May 21		Entrained for Southampton at 12.55 pm, train 10 x 3'9 from government siding, Aldershot. The whole station was loaded in half an hour without a hitch, horses gave no trouble whatever. We arrived at Southampton about 4 pm & watered the horses & entrained immediately. This was carried out in a satisfactory manner by the men. My horses were placed in two different positions on the same deck, the space that could have been occupied by my horses were afterwards filled with horses of other units, this condition of affairs necessitated me mounting two extra guards at one time, also six men for night guard. Having so few men at my disposal it made the work doubly arduous forage & rations for horses & men were carried on board ship. We left Southampton about 7 pm & lay about 2 miles out in Southampton water all the night & most part of the next day.	
	May 22		At 4 pm our journey for France commenced, being escorted by two	

Army Form C. 2118.

WAR DIARY
or
INTELLIGENCE SUMMARY.
(Erase heading not required.)

Instructions regarding War Diaries and Intelligence Summaries are contained in F. S. Regs., Part II. and the Staff Manual respectively. Title pages will be prepared in manuscript.

Place	Date	Hour	Summary of Events and Information	Remarks and references to Appendices
	May 22nd		torpedo destroyers. Our journey was uneventful. The water on board ship for the horses was not good, none of them drank a bucketful each. On starting SS with "Nouvelles (?)" it was unfit for ordinary purposes. The hay was a good transport, none of the deck. Harness was very hot & stuffy, all saddlery & harness were removed at the time of embarking, but was replaced the night before we arrived at Havre.	
	May 23rd		Arrived at Havre about 5 am. We started disembarking about 9 am. Two of my horses were sick & feverish, eating very little, all the rest were in excellent form. Disembarking was carried out without a hitch, not one horse had a bruise or a scrape as far as I viewed my orders from the M.L.O. I proceeded with a guard to No 5 Rest Camp. The horse lines were placed along side of the road, unfortunately a bad position, the horses being covered in dust, from motor lorries & other units passing down the road. Rations & forage were obtained, then entraining orders arrived	

WAR DIARY
or
INTELLIGENCE SUMMARY.
(Erase heading not required.)

Army Form C. 2118.

Place	Date	Hour	Summary of Events and Information	Remarks and references to Appendices
	May 23rd		Point 5 & our two marcheurs being the allotted place, had to to to point 4.30 am. Spent the few hours off and disposed resting, which was badly needed. Reveille to be at 3 am.	
	May 24th		Rise at 3 am. Watered horses & loaded up, & marched out at 4 am. Arrived at Point 5 at 4.30 am exactly. Off-saddled, reported to the R.T.O., saw our trucks both for horses & waggons, the former having the name of our unit written on in chalk, which simplified matters a great deal. Men got to work & loaded horses quickly, as the same time my sergeant & a party of men went and drew rations and days rations was received, not two days in accordance with orders received to on a printed form. Land was available to place on floors of wagons which was beneficial. Wagons were loaded with some difficulty as no room was left on the trucks which were occupied by the 4.3rd Field Ambulance however we managed to squeeze in half a limber & & three or thereabouts the	

Army Form C. 2118.

WAR DIARY
or
INTELLIGENCE SUMMARY.
(Erase heading not required.)

Instructions regarding War Diaries and Intelligence Summaries are contained in F. S. Regs., Part II. and the Staff Manual respectively. Title pages will be prepared in manuscript.

Place	Date	Hour	Summary of Events and Information	Remarks and references to Appendices
	May 24th		train. The time due to depart was 8.55 am, i.e. I had from 4.30 am until 7 am when the shunting began, to load two lumbers & 24 horses, a lot of time wasted walking about the station when one could have been resting. Horses & men at Camp. Breakfast was supplied to the men by a buffet managed by two ladies this was greatly appreciated. Two men were placed in each horse wagon, saddlery "forage" in the passage way. 8 horses per wagon. Wagons were supplied for the men no seats to sit on, straw would be supplied if no smoking of course. The men would rather another, as they sat on the straw wagon floor. Arrived at Monsieur Bowery at 3 pm. Horses were fed & watered, men obtained coffee supplied free of charge. Stayed an hour, then left for Abbeville, arriving there at 8 pm. Horses watered & fed again, hot water was available for the men to make tea. After half an hour's halt we started for Cassel arriving there at 5 am	

Army Form C. 2118.

WAR DIARY
or
INTELLIGENCE SUMMARY.
(Erase heading not required.)

Instructions regarding War Diaries and Intelligence Summaries are contained in F. S. Regs., Part II. and the Staff Manual respectively. Title pages will be prepared in manuscript.

Place	Date	Hour	Summary of Events and Information	Remarks and references to Appendices
	May 24th		Started to unload immediately we arrived, horses were ready in three quarters of an hour, but there was a great delay owing to the disposition of my waggons. Only a few could be unloaded at a time. Started out for Watten after an uneventful journey, no accidents occurred on the journey.	
	May 25th		Arrived at Watten about 12 noon, went to the billets which were allotted to me, & found a fairly good one for my horses, a small one at that, not a good place, as my horses had not laid down since leaving England on the 21st inst. no accommodation for my men or myself. Pointed out that facts to my A.D.V.S. We then found another farm called Selvas Farm, no accommodation in a big field for my horses & plenty of room for reception lines to accommodate the whole of our division. A good barn for my men. Unfortunately my horses had nothing to eat except a bale

Army Form C. 2118.

WAR DIARY
or
INTELLIGENCE SUMMARY.
(Erase heading not required.)

Place	Date	Hour	Summary of Events and Information	Remarks and references to Appendices
	May 25th		of hay which I brought with me. No rations could be supplied because the supply people knew nothing about our arrival, they had however have sick my rations in two days previously.	
	May 26th		Remained in Bullen. Collected some sick horses. Admitted two suffering from gangrenous Pneumonia, both of which died. Received orders to proceed to Broxelle the following day.	
	May 27th		Left for Broxelle at 2 p.m. Before leaving got word that two horses for the base were left at Bellegarde. I despatched a batman at 2 p.m. 4.3 men mounted to fetch these. They were up at Broxelle that night. As I had obtained a set of maps from the A.D.V.S this emptyed matters. I sent on the rest of the sick horses to M. Omer by an N.C.O. I gave him instructions to report to R.T.O. there for a billet for the night for men & horses, & to await the arrival of the other two who were collected from Bellegarde the following day. Arrived at Broxelle about 6 pm. no billets were allotted to us, as no billeting party was sent on that morning by mistake	

WAR DIARY
~~INTELLIGENCE SUMMARY~~
(Erase heading not required.)

Army Form C. 2118.

Instructions regarding War Diaries and Intelligence Summaries are contained in F.S. Regs., Part II and the Staff Manual respectively. Title pages will be prepared in manuscript.

Place	Date	Hour	Summary of Events and Information	Remarks and references to Appendices
	May 28th		Saw the main & advanced billets at Moulin Bateau. Later on the collecting party arrived at Belcee. Received orders to proceed to La Brayelle.	
	May 29th		Early in the morning. One horse was found tied to a tree outside the billet, no name of unit or a note was left with it. Sent on the remainder of the sick to the Road to St Omer by mounted men to join up with those washing there, gave them instructions to meet at La Brayelle. Went on a Bicycle party carrying of interpreter & one man. Left Broxeele & road for Cassel, arriving there about noon, halted near a mere watered, fed the horses & men had lunch. Started after half an hour for La Brayere, arriving there at 4 pm. found everything arranged for us by an interpreter. Collected horses. Slept behind by most of drivers, at Sylvester Deppe.	
	May 30th		Honneghem Colloiden. Spent day in Billets. General Review. Received orders to proceed to Westouter the following day. Sent on Bileeting party that night.	

1577 Wt.W10791/1773 500,000 1/15 D.D. & L. A.D.S.S./Forms/C. 2118.

WAR DIARY
or
INTELLIGENCE SUMMARY
(Erase heading not required.)

Army Form C. 2118.

Place	Date	Hour	Summary of Events and Information	Remarks and references to Appendices
	May 31st		Duty over to the trenches by Ebblinghem.	
	June 1st		Left for Westoutre at 9 am. Went via Cassel. Halted at 12 noon for an hour, fed horses in a field, and on out to refilling point then on up as at Westoutre at Westoutre about 4 pm. Put up two large sick lines. General Routine. Sent horses to the train from Godewaersvelde. My rich out was Easter and removing from my previous experience with the cavalry of the former station. I send an orderly train to find out if no could entrain sick horses there. This saves a lot of unnecessary fatigue for men & horses.	
	June 2nd		Visit by A.D.V.S. [signature] General Routine. Thinking Isabel to him something now, I keep a number of cases for treatment. Visit by A.D.V.S.	
	June 3rd			

Army Form C. 2118.

WAR DIARY
or
INTELLIGENCE SUMMARY.
(Erase heading not required.)

Instructions regarding War Diaries and Intelligence Summaries are contained in F. S. Regs., Part II. and the Staff Manual respectively. Title pages will be prepared in manuscript.

Place	Date	Hour	Summary of Events and Information	Remarks and references to Appendices
	June 4th		Routine as usual & attended conference at A.D.V.S. office	
	June 5th		" "	
	June 6th		Visit by A.D.V.S.	
			Sent an orderly to Yzeuwacker to arrange for 2 waggons	
	June 7th		Proceeding to the base the following day	
			Sick horses entrained for the base & routine as usual.	
	June 8th		Visit by A.D.V.S.	
	June 9th		Routine as usual.	
	June 10th		" "	
	June 11th		Routine as usual & attended conference at A.D.V.S. office	
	June 12th		" " a despatched an orderly to Yzeuwacker to arrange for 2 waggons	
			for horses proceeding to the base the following day.	
			Sick horses entrained for the base & routine as usual	
	June 13th		Routine as usual	
	June 14th		" " despatched an orderly to Yzeuwacker to arrange for waggons for horses proceeding to the base the following day.	

Army Form C. 2118.

WAR DIARY
or
INTELLIGENCE SUMMARY.
(Erase heading not required.)

Instructions regarding War Diaries and Intelligence Summaries are contained in F. S. Regs., Part II. and the Staff Manual respectively. Title pages will be prepared in manuscript.

Place	Date	Hour	Summary of Events and Information	Remarks and references to Appendices
	Nov 15th		Received orders to move at once; the proved to Billey between attack & Watou. Sick horses entrained for the train. Arrived at Billey, good accommodation for all.	
	16th		Routine as usual	
	17th		" " "	
	18th		Despatched a party to Godewaersvelde to collect horses left there by the Divisions. Attended conference at A.D.V.S. Office	
	19th		Routine as usual	
	20th		" " "	
	21st		Received orders to proceed to Middelkerke about 1½ miles. Despatches an orderly to Godewaersvelde to arrange for 2 waggons for horses proceeding with has the following day. Arrived at Middelk. good accommodation for all. Sick horses entrained for the train.	
	22nd		Routine as usual	
	23rd		" " "	
	24th		Routine as usual; attended conference at A.D.V.S. Office	
	25th			

Army Form C. 2118.

WAR DIARY
or
INTELLIGENCE SUMMARY.
(Erase heading not required.)

Place	Date	Hour	Summary of Events and Information	Remarks and references to Appendices
	Jun 26th		Routine as usual	
	27th		" " "	
	28th		" " "	
	29th		Despatched a party to collect horses of westoutre, famed they were collected by No 5 Mobile Vety. Section. Routine as usual	
	30th		Routine as usual	

T.J. Wiston Lieut
O.C. 26th Mobile Vety Section

14th Division

121/6401

26th Mobile Vety. Section.

Vol: II

1-31-7-15

Army Form C. 2118.

WAR DIARY
or
INTELLIGENCE SUMMARY.
(Erase heading not required.)

Instructions regarding War Diaries and Intelligence Summaries are contained in F. S. Regs., Part II and the Staff Manual respectively. Title pages will be prepared in manuscript.

Place	Date	Hour	Summary of Events and Information	Remarks and references to Appendices
In the Field	July 1st		Routine as usual	
	2nd		Despatched a party to collect horses at Westampnes. Attended conference at A.D.V.S. Office & received information that this Division had been sending to the base, the least number of horses for the past few weeks, by the returns are not well ahead. Enquired from A.S.W.C. if it been not possible to exchange Transport Waggons, as two timbers are insufficient to carry equipment of section & one days forage for horses. The number of oats & hay, fill one limber, & then one has the other limber for the rest of gear. I noticed that all other stations that I have met, have a F.S. waggon & spring cart. Routine as usual. Sick horses despatched to the Base.	
	3rd			
	4th		Routine as usual, saddlery & Rifle inspection, both very good & in good condition	

WAR DIARY
or
INTELLIGENCE SUMMARY.
(Erase heading not required.)

Army Form C. 2118.

Place	Date	Hour	Summary of Events and Information	Remarks and references to Appendices
In the Field	July 5th		Dispatched an orderly to Godewaersvelde to arrange for two wagons for the sick horses being sent to the base. Had the following class of horses in splendid condition. Have a fair number of horses on hand undergoing treatment, some too lame to do the journey to Railhead, & others which will be cured in a few days time.	
	6th		Routine as usual. Visit from A.D.V.S. Sick horses despatched to the base.	
	7th		Paid a visit to Ordnance stores to enquire about material ordered for about a month ago. Nothing to do yet. Routine as usual.	
	8th		Routine as usual. Built a field oven, as the farmer's wife has taken down his oven so that we could not use it. The oven was a complete success. It was composed of a brick bottom & a dome made of biscuit tins covered with a layer of clay.	
	9th		Routine as usual. Attended conference with A.D.V.S. Officer i/c. P.m. held an inclue with stick on tom-tom.	
	10th		Routine as usual. A mare belonging to transport Sergeant of Wesleyan Press (6th Chaplain L.S.) died of colic. History of frequent attacks of colic. A disposition obvious (point & fracture of lumbar vertebrae) by was ablated by broken land.	

Army Form C. 2118.

WAR DIARY
or
INTELLIGENCE SUMMARY.
(Erase heading not required.)

Instructions regarding War Diaries and Intelligence Summaries are contained in F.S. Regs., Part II. and the Staff Manual respectively. Title pages will be prepared in manuscript.

Place	Date	Hour	Summary of Events and Information	Remarks and references to Appendices
In the field	July 10th		before, as I was interested in the case, I made a Post mortem to see if a calculus was present, found a very acute enteritis confined to the double colon, the contents were ligneous probably due to the strecline (?) given during the day. The P.M. was most interesting for the men as it was an opportunity to give them a lecture as the same time. The unfortunate part about it was that we were minus the P.M. instruments, so we had to manage with what we could find to answer the purpose. Despatches an orderly to Todmorden to arrange for two trucks for sick horses being sent to the base on Monday.	
	11th		Routine as usual & saddlery & Rifle inspection.	
	12th		Routine as usual. Horses despatched to the base. One man with a turn on O Neck fell down, lay there all day, the men turning it over when occasion required.	
	13th		Routine as usual. Managed to get more up, which fell down yesterday. Made a set of slings out of two posts, a rug, head rope & wound ropes of my waggon, also the kitchen & bread straps of the harness. He now looks quite a thing him.	

Army Form C. 2118.

WAR DIARY
or
INTELLIGENCE SUMMARY.
(Erase heading not required.)

Instructions regarding War Diaries and Intelligence Summaries are contained in F. S. Regs., Part II. and the Staff Manual respectively. Title pages will be prepared in manuscript.

Place	Date	Hour	Summary of Events and Information	Remarks and references to Appendices
In the Field	July 14th		Routine changed as follows:-	
			Reveille 5.30 am	
			Exercise 6.0 am to 7.15 am	
			Water & Feed 7.30	
			Breakfast 7.45	
			Parade 9. am	
			Stables 9.10 am (all horses groomed including sick, general clean up lines etc.)	
			Break 10.0 am	
			Stables 11.30 am	
			Water & Feed 12.45 am	
			Dinner 1.0 pm	
			Stables 2.30 pm (Fatigues cleaning lines etc)	
			Water & Feed 5.0 pm	
			Tea 5.30 pm	
	15th		Horse admitted with Tetanus, belonging to 42nd Field Ambulance Corps. Visit from D.D.V.S. & A.D.V.S. Have to take charge of the 5th Corps Hdqrs also I.R. Workshops horses. Routine as above as I am the only V.O. available.	

WAR DIARY or INTELLIGENCE SUMMARY

Army Form C. 2118.

Place	Date	Hour	Summary of Events and Information	Remarks and references to Appendices
In the Field	July 16th		Routine as usual. Attended conference of A.D.V.S. officers.	
	17th		" " Despatched an orderly to Gouzeaucourt to arrange for two wagons for horses being sent to the base the following day. Horse parade of 5th Corps H'gtrs at 10.30 a.m.	
	18th		" " Horses sent to the base from Gouzeaucourt, as this station is now being used for troops as most horses can be despatched from this station. I elected one horse & examined 51 motor the rest.	
	19th			
	20th		Paid a visit to 5th Both Stead'gmirs also R.E. workshop 6th Corps to inspect horses belonging to them.	
	21st		Routine as usual.	
	22nd		" "	

Army Form C. 2118.

WAR DIARY
or
INTELLIGENCE SUMMARY.
(Erase heading not required.)

Instructions regarding War Diaries and Intelligence Summaries are contained in F.S. Regs., Part II. and the Staff Manual respectively. Title pages will be prepared in manuscript.

Place	Date	Hour	Summary of Events and Information	Remarks and references to Appendices
In the field	July 23rd		Routine as usual. Went to 21/6 Section for conference. It was most interesting & we debay doing the new method of treating for glanders, injecting Mallein under the skin of lower eyelid. Did I myself afterwards, & I should think it very practical as no temperature has to be taken.	
	24th		Routine as usual.	
	25th		" " Had a loan of horse ambulance, managed to procure a cattle wagon from a farmer at Warton as the rate of 2/6 per day. This will be very useful for bringing horses from the various units when occasion arises, but I think it would be unwise to use it for despatching horses from here to the railhead. Despatched horses to the Breathe from entraining to the base, a distance of about 15 kilometres. Received a wire from A.D.V.S. saying the new fellow did not arrive at Villet, very	
	26a		from Nicemeyshym. Received orders to proceed to Warton to procure an ambulance. Stayed night, order to go to gaivainville to arrange for two wagons from there & had to go to Calabre according to orders received from R.T.O. & Separation from stable (have two horses unable to walk. Could	Impossible to open line at 5.45 a/p. m 10-35 a. m
	26b			Because the horse happens to be not very tall it will still be without help a long sniff.

1577 Wt. W10791/1773 500,000 1/15 D. D. & L. A.D.S.S./Forms/C. 2118.

Army Form C. 2118.

WAR DIARY
or
INTELLIGENCE SUMMARY.
(Erase heading not required.)

Place	Date	Hour	Summary of Events and Information	Remarks and references to Appendices
L. Nuffield	July 26th		Poor place. Refugees the only occupants. The place did not belong to things. Went about 600 yds down the road, found a nice farm's good accommodation for all.	
	27th		Routine as usual. Got settled down. Everything finished before Nightfall. Built oven, different pattern, frame for Stretches on top. Frame in Centre & oven sunk in the earth.	
	28th		Routine as usual. Built Kitchen around oven half a timber on its end with 3 divisions as shelves, the covers were utilized for heavy coverings. Wiring from A.D.S. the whole arrangements. He also was very pleased with the whole arrangements. He also suggested an advanced post, which will necessitate two men going forward beyond Poperinghe, on this place is rather far back, there men will take over the horses from Units at Vlamertinghe, Ypres, & conduct them back to here.	
	29th		Routine as usual. Had a wire from A.D.V.S. that the D.D.V.S. would be there at 3 p.m. for some unknown reason, he did not come.	

WAR DIARY
or
INTELLIGENCE SUMMARY.
(Erase heading not required.)

Army Form C. 2118.

Place	Date	Hour	Summary of Events and Information	Remarks and references to Appendices
In Field	July 30		Went to Steele. Horse parade of 5th Coy. Stages & R.E. worked boys. Attended conference at D.D.S. Office. Routine as usual.	
	31		Routine as usual. Pond in field used in to prevent battle & hogs from fouling the water supply. Completed washing trough for men. Managed to obtain some ties for use as washing basin. Arranged for a small house for men to bath in. Also for disposal of manure. Visit from D.D.V.S. He was very pleased with the idea of limber on its end (the centre boards placed in as shelves) being as a cupboard for my kitchen. Despatched an orderly to Jacatre to arrange for two wagons for Monday for the disposal of sick horses to the base.	

J.J. Weir Major.
O.C. 26 Mobile Vety Section

121/6753

14th Division

26th Mobile Vet: Section.
Vol: III
August 15

Army Form C. 2118.

WAR DIARY
or
INTELLIGENCE SUMMARY.
(Erase heading not required.)

Instructions regarding War Diaries and Intelligence Summaries are contained in F.S. Regs., Part II. and the Staff Manual respectively. Title pages will be prepared in manuscript.

Place	Date	Hour	Summary of Events and Information	Remarks and references to Appendices
In the Field	Aug 25th		Routine as usual.	
	26th		Routine as usual. Attended to horse belonging to S.L.I. which was very lame.	
	27th		Routine as usual. Attended conference at A.D.V.S's Office. On arrival home I heard that one of my Lumbers had broken wheels coming from Ytypres with stones. I owned an abandoned half of Lumber at La Faux tu Bryan, had it brought to billet, took all fittings off other Lumber & fitted up the abandoned one. View from A.D.V.S. & Divisionary Officer. Both very pleased with the whole arrangement.	
	28th		Routine as usual. Dispatched an orderly to Divisional HQ to arrange for two trucks for horses to proceed to the base the following day.	
	29th		Routine as usual. Dispatched sick horses to base.	
	30th		Routine as usual.	
	31st		Routine as usual. Wire from A.D.V.S.	

J.W. McLaren
O.C.

26th MOBILE VETERINARY SECTION

WAR DIARY
or
INTELLIGENCE SUMMARY.
(Erase heading not required.)

Army Form C. 2118.

Place	Date	Hour	Summary of Events and Information	Remarks and references to Appendices
In the Field	Aug 1st		Attended Horse parade at 5th Corps Hdqts. Routine as usual. Despatched two men to W.O.6 mobile Vety Section as an advanced post.	
	2nd		Sick horses despatched to Base Hospital. Routine as usual.	
	3rd		Visit the 5th Corps & Cornwall R.E. Attended an urgent case at 112 T. S. of E. Horse very bad with Colic, gave 1½ arecoline hypodermically. The horse died about half an hour afterwards. The arecoline had not the desired effect.	
	4th		Routine as usual.	
	5th		Visit to 5th Corps Hdqtrs & Cornwall R.E. Transferred one of their horses to my section for disposal to the Base. Attended parade with S.D.R. for the transfer of surplus horses from 5th Corps. Leaving from A.D.V.S.	
	6th		Attended conference at A.D.V.S. office. Held P.M. on horse destroyed with picked up nail, found joint full of pus.	
	7th		Went to 14. S. of E. Held P.M. on a charger which had died suddenly. The Officer rode it from Ypres when he arrived at B.E.M. the horse was very ill, temperature 106°. Cause of death was the stomach was full of Botts Gastrophilus equi(?) to fabulous(?) amounts. A reference stomach found which was covered internally a great army of them. Gastrophilus is never a danger for troops was awaked (?)	

26th MOBILE VETERINARY SECTION

Army Form C. 2118.

WAR DIARY
or
INTELLIGENCE SUMMARY.
(Erase heading not required.)

Instructions regarding War Diaries and Intelligence Summaries are contained in F. S. Regs., Part II. and the Staff Manual respectively. Title pages will be prepared in manuscript.

Place	Date	Hour	Summary of Events and Information	Remarks and references to Appendices
In the field	May 8th		Visit to 5th Coy. & R.E. troughs for Water troughs (wooden) and turned by 3 & 4 3.0.8. through N.V.V.S. each costs 8 frcs. Dispatched men with my left horses for Remount Depot. Visit by 29. V. V. S.	
	9th		Despatched men to Remount Depot for any 10 mules to replace our own which were killed & wounded belonging to Divnl. Coy of Infantry. Horses despatched to base Hospital. Arrival ambulance for the removal of two horses which could not walk. To Railhead.	
	10th		Visit to 5th Coy. & R.E. Routine as usual	
	11th		Routine as usual.	
	12th		Routine as usual. Lost a man : List a man for 8 frcs moved to two small.	
	13th		Attended conference at at. J. V. S. Office. Routine as usual. Received water troughs 6ft long x 1ft deep	
	14th		Routine as usual.	

WAR DIARY or INTELLIGENCE SUMMARY

Army Form C. 2118.

Place	Date	Hour	Summary of Events and Information	Remarks and references to Appendices
In the Field	16th		Inspection in morning to endeavour to arrange for two trucks to convey sick horses to Base Horse Parade by 5th Batt. Hodgson. Visit from A.D.V.S. Horses despatched to Base hospital. Three ambulance convoys come home to Railhead, which came in awaits. Two others transferred on to No 12 Veterinary Hospital.	
	17th		Visit to 5th Batt. R.E. Made arrangements for a few leaves to build up the sides of my trenches. Forwarded an addl/to R.E. about wooden ages, I have not heard anything of X arrived ago. New stone to drag up the you wagon to drag stones from Poperinghe for the purpose of making floors for stables. Many had ratstrong etc. The wells contain water enough then been drawn. Held P.M. on a mare which I traced to a mouth anthrax from the joint, very interesting. Horse admitted with wounded knee in great pain this at 5.30 P.M. P.M. tomorrow.	
	18th		Made approach to Kitchen out of bacon boxes. Had to remove limber as it was required for drawing stones from Poperinghe. Relieved of charge of 5th Batt. Waggon R.E. Visit from A.D.V.S. Held P.M. on horse which died yesterday. Over 500 ducks telemetry for horses of the division	

1577 Wt. W10791/1773 500,000 1/15 D. D. & L. A.D.S.S./Forms/C. 2118.

Army Form C. 2118.

WAR DIARY
or
INTELLIGENCE SUMMARY.
(Erase heading not required.)

Instructions regarding War Diaries and Intelligence Summaries are contained in F. S. Regs., Part II. and the Staff Manual respectively. Title pages will be prepared in manuscript.

Place	Date	Hour	Summary of Events and Information	Remarks and references to Appendices
In the Field	Aug 19th		Routine as usual. Found some difficulty in trying to draw mounts as have to revert to the old process of starching with basil, covering with sacks for five days, then the wood, & arrange it.	
	20th		Went to conference at A.D.V.S. office. Routine as usual	
	21st		Routine as usual.	
	22nd		Despatched an orderly to Goudewaerde to arrange for two wagons to convey sick horses to the train, strong ambulance & despatched to convey sick horses, very lame, from 45th R.J.A. West to Vlamertinghe to train back recalled, because No 6 Station have moved near Poperinghe from A.D.V.S.) men of advanced post recalled, because No 6 Station have moved near Poperinghe Horses despatched to base hospital, also to Remount Depot. Routine as usual	
	23rd			
	24th		Found a suitable place for any water-stable about 20 yds from the road, as it is essential not to go too far into a field, or it becomes one sea of mud in the winter weather. The bricking of stables is putting down a good solid stone floor, this will take at least a month to complete.	

1577 Wt.W10791/1773 500,000 1/15 D. D. & L.   A.D.S.S./Forms/C. 2118.

121/6923

14th Division

26th Mobile Vet: Section

vol. IV.

Sept. 15

WAR DIARY
INTELLIGENCE SUMMARY
(Erase heading not required.)

Army Form C. 2118.

Instructions regarding War Diaries and Intelligence Summaries are contained in F.S. Regs., Part II. and the Staff Manual respectively. Title pages will be prepared in manuscript.

Place	Date	Hour	Summary of Events and Information	Remarks and references to Appendices
In the Field	1st September		Routine as usual. Visit by A.D.V.S. Shed going ahead with stable	
	2nd "		Routine as usual.	
	3rd "		Routine as usual. Removed horses from old lines as they were up to their hocks in mud, through the weather we have been having lately.	
	4th "		Routine as usual. Saddlery & Rifle inspection. Despatched an orderly to Gonnevieville to arrange for two wagons, for sick horses proceeding to the base tomorrow. Floor of stable nearly complete.	
	5th "		Despatched horse to Gonnevieville. Horse ambulance so that I could get two lame Mules to Railhead. Visit by D.D.V.S. Received orders to collect horses in the vicinity of Sastre.	
	6th "		Routine as usual.	
	7th "		Routine as usual. Stable floor finished. Labourers for some beams & lathing for floor & roof.	

WAR DIARY
INTELLIGENCE SUMMARY.
(Erase heading not required.)

Army Form C. 2118.

Place	Date	Hour	Summary of Events and Information	Remarks and references to Appendices
In the Field	7th	Sept/9	Routine as usual. Visit by A.D.V.S.	
	9th		Started off at 9 am to collect horses belonging to the 33rd Division at Hondeghem. Dispatched the sick ones to the sick convoy. Sent over to my section. Obtained at least went to R.T.O. & arranged for Wagons then to the supply Officer to arrange for supplies for men & horses. The horses were moved at the head the following day.	
	10th		Dispatched sick animals to E centre to join up with those that I left the previous day.	
	11th		Routine as usual. Received orders to inform my superiors that he was recalled to the French Mission for duty.	
	12th		Routine as usual. Inoculing ? Rifle inspection.	
	13th		Routine as usual. Semi-Famines. Used to furnish the labor off.	
	14th		Routine as usual. Dispatched an orderly to ? wagons for two wagons for sick animals proceeding to the ? the following day.	

Army Form C. 2118.

WAR DIARY
or
INTELLIGENCE SUMMARY.
(Erase heading not required.)

Instructions regarding War Diaries and Intelligence Summaries are contained in F. S. Regs., Part II. and the Staff Manual respectively. Title pages will be prepared in manuscript.

Place	Date	Hour	Summary of Events and Information	Remarks and references to Appendices
In the field	15th	left	Despatched sick animals to the midhead. Work on stables continued. Got a railway leading to stables & filled in with stones.	
	16th "		Routine as usual. I now have the 4.6" Bde R.F.A. under my charge whilst their V.O. is on leave.	
	17th "		Routine as usual. Visit 70 & 6th Bde R.F.A. Attended conference at S.D.V.S. office.	
	18th "		Routine as usual.	
	19th "		Routine as usual. Saddlery & R.F.4. inspection. Despatched an enemy to gooseneck to arrange for wagons.	
	20th "		Despatched sick animals to Railhead.	
	21st "		Routine as usual.	
	22nd "		Continue as usual.	
	23rd "		Routine as usual. Visit from A.D.V.S.	
	24th "		Routine as usual. Attended conference at S.D.V.S. office.	

1577 Wt. W10791/1773 500,000 1/15 D. D. & L. A.D.S.S./Forms/C. 2118.

Army Form C. 2118

WAR DIARY
or
INTELLIGENCE SUMMARY.
(Erase heading not required.)

Place	Date	Hour	Summary of Events and Information	Remarks and references to Appendices
In the Field	25th Sept.		Routine as usual.	
	26th "		Routine as usual. Rifle inspection. I have arranged for Saddlery inspection to be on Tuesday as we generally have a lot of sick animals to look after about the end of the week. I expected an evacuation about tomorrow. I gave half of my section a half holiday every Sunday from 2 pm to 9 pm, as they are kept very busy all the week attending stables etc. arrange for trucks.	
	27th "		Despatched sick animals to the Railhead. Routine as usual.	
	28th "		Routine as usual. Saddlery inspection.	
	29th "		Routine as usual.	
	30th "		Routine as usual.	

J G Willis Dare
OC
26th Mobile Veterinary Section
30.9.15

12/7594

14th Hussars

26th Noti: Vet: Sect:
Vol: 5

Oct 15

WAR DIARY

INTELLIGENCE SUMMARY

Army Form C. 21

Place	Date	Hour	Summary of Events and Information	Remarks and references to Appendices
Watou	1/10/15		Routine as usual.	
"	2nd		Routine as usual.	
"	3rd		The G.O.C. 1st Division, paid an unexpected visit a.t.p.m., he was interested in the shell cases, + was anxious to know as many horses as affected there been admitted since our arrival in this country, + what was the general result. Fortunately so far we have had a very low percentage of shot injuries, + of course none of them have shed Anti-titanic serum is injected on arrival in the section, as I have also example of horses belonging to other units affected with tetanus from shell wounds, + have heard that it is prevalent. All cases of horses up until admitted to the course Anti-titanic serum, + up to now no cases of tetanus have occurred, + needless to add the greatest proportion of them have been very bad cases.	
"	4th		S.E Pte [?] Raymond G. transferred to U.C. reinforcements Rouen. S.E Pte Wilson W. to No 19 Vety Hospital Rouen. Saddle + rifle inspection. Routine as usual. Unit moved to Godevaersvelde to order bare magnet to [?]	
"	5th		Sick horses sent to the base. Five in number. Visit by A.D.V.S. he is arranging to have a wooden cookhouse, latrine, + a hut for the men as read inasmuch as weather for me. The men are living in a barn, + as the days are getting shorter, a place must be found for them to read to smoke, as the latter is strictly forbidden in the barn.	
"	6th		Routine as usual. Very few sick horses. Work in stables continued.	
"	7th		Routine as usual.	
"	8th		Went to conference at A.D.V.S.S. office Vlamertinghe. Col. Wilson D.D.V.S. 2nd Army called	

Army Form C. 2118

WAR DIARY
or
INTELLIGENCE SUMMARY.
(Erase heading not required.)

Instructions regarding War Diaries and Intelligence Summaries are contained in F. S. Regs., Part II. and the Staff Manual respectively. Title pages will be prepared in manuscript.

26th MOBILE VETERINARY SECTION

Place	Date	Hour	Summary of Events and Information	Remarks and references to Appendices
Watou	8th		and tied up about a dozen of mules resembling Epizootic Lymphangitis; I rendered having a case at Westoutre similar, a negative result was obtained with Mallein. Mule was returned to its unit; the nodules on both hind legs followed the course of the lymphatic vessels, but no enteric in skin or when was noticed in this particular case.	
Watou	9th		Routine as usual. Sent to VLAMERTINGHE for brides, having borrowed two G.S. wagons from D.A.C. Went to 46th Brigade R.F.A. & destroyed a horse suffering from Tetanus. The result of a shell wound. I have its companion in my section, from which I removed three pieces of shell, another one entered the abdomen, she is showing no bad signs as a result.	
Watou	10th		Saddlery rifle inspection. Visit by A.D.V.S. Routine as usual.	
"	11th		Sent orderly to Godeversvelde to arrange for wagons. Six horses arrive from 48th Brig. R.F.A. with shell wounds, some very bad cases. Busy removing pieces of shell and injecting Anti-tetanic Serum.	
"	12th		Sick horses sent to the base. Ten in number.	
"	13th		Four bootsies arrive for the men, had them dyed Khaki, + rested. Routine as usual.	
"	14th		Reveille is now at 6 a.m. not 5.30 a.m. as before, as everything is corresponding by	

Army Form C. 2118

WAR DIARY
or
INTELLIGENCE SUMMARY.
(Erase heading not required.)

Instructions regarding War Diaries and Intelligence Summaries are contained in F. S. Regs., Part II. and the Staff Manual respectively. Title pages will be prepared in manuscript.

Place	Date	Hour	Summary of Events and Information	Remarks and references to Appendices
Walin	14th		started. Sent to Vlamertinghe for bricks, expert on floor portable, as the cement is a failure being too brittle.	
"	15.		Visit by A.D.V.S. Routine covered.	
"	16.		Routine as usual. Have taken over charge of the 4th 3rd Brig Iny Transport puppy Meike who is in order	
"	17.		Saddlery rifle that inspection. P.M. held on a horse belonging to D.L.O. Yeomanry have septic arthritis elbow joint the result of a kick. Visit Infantry Transport.	
"	18th		Sent to R.E Park Vlamertinghe for cement, + to St. Jans Ter Begen for several bricks as being laid down on the leach also with a opente of cement, & liquid cement proved in, this I think will solve the floor question. Went to Proven district and collected one mule of the 2/4 L. Division. Visit the infantry transport in way home. Sent a man to Goduaersvelde to arrange for wagons.	
"	19.		Sent horses to the base eleven in number. Visit by A.D.V.S. Visit infantry transport	
"	20.		Sent two wagons to Vlamertinghe for bricks, could only fill one as the shells were coming too thick to wait for more. Visit to the Infantry Transport.	

Army Form C. 2118.

WAR DIARY
or
INTELLIGENCE SUMMARY.
(Erase heading not required.)

Instructions regarding War Diaries and Intelligence Summaries are contained in F. S. Regs., Part II. and the Staff Manual respectively. Title pages will be prepared in manuscript.

Place	Date	Hour	Summary of Events and Information	Remarks and references to Appendices
Watou	21/1/-		Routine as usual. Forty nine Remounts arrive for the Division	
"	22nd		Went to Conference at A.D.V.S's Office Vlamertinghe. Visit by A.D.V.S. in the morning, when the Remounts are exhibited.	
"	23rd		Sent to Proven for Mules. Routine as usual.	
"	24th		Saddlery rifle inspection visit by the A.D.V.S. 9 Mule received to meet Reinforcement at Poperinghe, sent men mounted leading horses to meet them, the N.C.O. was told that they were taken off the train at Casselle. Horses returned from field into stable as it is raining hard. Plenty of new drawn hair placed in Cap of the Mules. Sent men mounted to meet reinforcements at Casselle. Went to Abele to Field Cashier to Pay NCO's & Men. Sent orderly to Godewaersvelde to arrange for wagons. The men for remounts to arrive.	
"	25th			
"	26th		1 Sergt, 1 Corporal, & 5 men from No.7 Vety Hospital. 1 Sergt, 1 Corporal & 5 men sent to No.7. Vety Hospital in exchange for those who arrived yesterday. Seven horses sent to Base. One wagon sent for same to Saint Jans Ter Bizen.	
"	27-		Sent two wagons to Proven for Mules. Routine as usual.	
"	28th		Routine as usual.	

WAR DIARY
or
INTELLIGENCE SUMMARY.

Army Form C. 2118

Place	Date	Hour	Summary of Events and Information	Remarks and references to Appendices
Watou	29th		Floor of stable completed with bricks. Horses are looking 50% better since stabled. Rugs have been issued, but are not used in the stable. Sick lines in a bad state, horses removed into the farm. Went to conference A.D.V.S.S. Ypres. This will now be held on the last Friday of every month.	
"	30th		Routine as usual.	
"	31st		One wagon sent to Poperinghe for Ordnance Stores, & one wagon to Abeele for sawdust & fine wood. Raining hard, so all outside work discontinued.	

F.J. Wei[?]
Lt. R.V.C.
O.C.

26th MOBILE VETERINARY SECTION
Date 31/10/15

14th Burann

26th Feb-Sep.
Vol: 6

1/31/7693

avp

Nov. 15

WAR DIARY
or
~~INTELLIGENCE SUMMARY~~

Army Form C. 2118

Place	Date	Hour	Summary of Events and Information	Remarks and references to Appendices
Watou	Nov 1st		Sent to Abele Saw mill for sawdust & pine wood, the other wagon went to orphanage Sisters Poperinghe. Routine as usual.	
"	2nd		Sent two wagons G.S. (lent by the D.A.C.) to R.E. Park Vlamertinghe for wood. Built a sick lines, cook house, latrine, & a hut for the men.	
"	3rd		Sent to Vlamertinghe one lurry wagon to draw corrugated iron for the roofing. Laid out plans for sick lines, put close it close to my own stable, connecting it both latter by means of a passage way. Sent an orderly to Godevaersvelde to order wagons for sick horses to remount.	
	4th		Sent horses to the bains, eight in number. Routine as usual.	
	5th		Routine as usual.	
	6th		Corporal Roberts promoted to sergeant from 30th October.	
	7th		Saddle rifle inspection, have a good number of sick for treatment. Started on sick lines building in the afternoon.	
	8th		Sent some men to Caestre Ry. Station to fetch remounts. I distributed same as they did not arrive until late in the evening, the A.D.V.S gave me the list of units requiring same.	

WAR DIARY
or
INTELLIGENCE SUMMARY

(Erase heading not required.)

Army Form C. 2.

Place	Date	Hour	Summary of Events and Information	Remarks and references to Appendices
Watou	9th Mar.		Sergt. Roberts and Pte Mitchell proceed to England on leave. Pouring rain, fair the waterproof sheet supplied for men's huts over the sick aisle to keep the floor dry as I have no linoleum to do same properly. Bourgignie sick tunes into the pantry made a little.	
"	10:		Building continued. Routine as usual. It is proposed to take away one limber from the section, from experience this is absurd, as the baggage, equipment + one days ration for men + horses would not fit in two limbers hence I had the sides raised one foot by means of boards. It is said that one does not require to carry any rations, the supply wagon should come every evening into camp(s); before leaving every man should get two days ration in his havresack, the corn for horse is 10 rations; I can quite imagine, catting up a first of beef and judgement man his lb of same, with cheese, bread, tea + sugar. I can quite see what it would be like in the evening, when each man produces his ration again; will the G.S. linger with supplies full as every evening I doubt it. Nothing is carried in excess. I 1098.89. until the following the upturn	

WAR DIARY
or
INTELLIGENCE SUMMARY.

(Erase heading not required.)

Army Form C. 2

Place	Date	Hour	Summary of Events and Information	Remarks and references to Appendices
Watou	Nov 10th		A mess tent for myself, a bell tent for each sergeant, + a few tents + a van for the company men.	
"	11th		Sent to Vlamertinghe for breakfast with two G.S. wagons borrowed from D.A.C. Major Bartlett, Lt Mahony myself were judges at the 4 & 2nd Inf. Brig. Shows. Everything was splendidly turned out, the 9th R. Brig. taking most of the prizes. The harness, wagons mules were as good as one could see even during peace time.	
	12th		A fearful gale blowing, the roof of my stable looked like blowing off, I got reinforcing beams put up immediately. The watchpump electric blew up here also. Sent nine sick horses to the base.	
	13rd		Visit by A.D.V.S. Routine as usual.	
	14th		Saddle rifle + kit inspection. Routine as usual.	
	15th		Sent to Poperinghe for ordnance stores. Building continued. Routine as usual.	

WAR DIARY
or
INTELLIGENCE SUMMARY.

(Erase heading not required.)

Army Form C. 2

Instructions regarding War Diaries and Intelligence Summaries are contained in F. S. Regs., Part II. and the Staff Manual respectively. Title pages will be prepared in manuscript.

Place	Date	Hour	Summary of Events and Information	Remarks and references to Appendices
Watou	Nov 16th		Sent to Vlamertinghe for wood. Routine as usual.	
"	" 17		Sent to Abele for sawdust & led down the horses.	
"	" 18th		Parade full marching order at 11 a.m. Inspection by the A.D.V.S. (Col Woaw) 2nd Army & the A.D.V.S. the A.D.V.S was pleased with the turn out.	
"	" 19th		Sixteen sick horses sent to the Base. Sent for a load of sand to St Jans ter Biezen.	
"	" 20		Sent to Vlamertinghe for corrugated iron, they had none, but they supplied me with rolls of ordinary canvas, & some wooden [?] for roofing.	
"	21		Sent to Poperinghe for coal. Work on hut commenced.	
"	22		Saddle & rifle inspection. Went to St Jans Ter Biezen to arrange for a shelter for orderly. This horse was re-injured. Went to Abele in the afternoon to draw money to pay my men. Visit by A.D.V.S., who probably came remounts which had arrived about twenty minutes before. Sent for sand to St Jans Ter Biezen to put a floor of rubble.	
"	23		Remedies to look with wooden floor &c & large cattle room is about 3/4 ft alignment	

WAR DIARY
or
INTELLIGENCE SUMMARY.

(Erase heading not required.)

Army Form C. 2118

Place	Date	Hour	Summary of Events and Information	Remarks and references to Appendices
Watou	Nov 25th		Sent for Sawdust to Abele, also a memo asking the O.C. if the Sawmill, if he will open up some tea leaves into planks for me. This he will do in a week's time. Started building a new cookhouse. Sent to St. Jans ten Bezen for sand. Sergt. Harrison leaves the Section - at his own request - in transfer to the M.T. row Cavalry Brigade Mobile Section. Sergt. Campbell takes over his duties & Sergt. Roberts becomes D.M.S. this will be a success as the latter is very willing to learn the clerical portion of the work of a Mobile Section, to being a proficient driver.	
"	26th		Routine as usual. Sent orderly to Godewaersvelde to order wagons for tomorrow.	
"	27th		Went to the conference at A.D.V.S.'s Office Flamertinghe. Eleven ambulances evacuated to the Base. The ambulance made two journeys, so that two very him cases which were unable to walk. Sent to Poperinghe for coal & ordnance stores.	
"	28th		No Saddle inspection held as 2 men invented every Friday to the Base this inspection will take place every Tuesday.	

WAR DIARY
INTELLIGENCE SUMMARY

Place	Date	Hour	Summary of Events and Information	Remarks and references to Appendices
Wadi	Nov 29th		A motor lorry kindly sent to me by the O.C. Am. Sub. Park cells & takes my teams to the Saw mills at Atele; the work was completed in the afternoon	
"	" 30th		Saddle rifle inspection; Floor of hut finished. Visit by the A.D.V.S.	

26 in Rub: Feb, Deck,
Vol: 7

12/7911

14th Brown

WAR DIARY
INTELLIGENCE SUMMARY

Army Form C. 2118.

Place	Date	Hour	Summary of Events and Information	Remarks and references to Appendices
In Salou	1/12/15		Routine as usual.	
	2nd		Work on cookhouse hut continued, floor of latrine completed. Routine carried on. Sick lines full of cases for evacuation to morrow. Sent an orderly to Hydrocarbonville to order 11 wagons. Tent raised 3/ft 6 ins from the ground, with sandbags, without wooden floor bottom, very comfortable. Lt Steele goes on leave to England. I take over charge of No. 9 Div Train, A.S.C. + Div Cavalry. Sent to C.R.E. for wood or corrugated iron to complete sick lines roof & cook house. They promise 9' x 3' sheets	
	3rd		I will have to get same at Steele sawmills. Routine as usual.	
	4th			
	5th		Thirty three horses sent to base, all the units are now sending in their sick cases fearing a move. Very busy, can just water & feed them—slings wounds to nurse. Sent with Lt Cowan with the news that the horses of the 46th Brig R.F.A. are to be mullewed	

WAR DIARY

Army Form C. 2118.

Place	Date	Hour	Summary of Events and Information	Remarks and references to Appendices
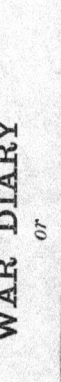	5th		at once. Lt Lewis myself start on "C" Battery at 2.p.m., finishing at 3.p.m. The new test (Intradermal Palpebral) was the one we used & found that a large proportion of the horses were done without even been held, in some cases where the horses were very restive, if found it better to let nobody near his head but myself + in this way succeeded. One syringe full was sufficient for 28 horses. It is a splendid method, so simple, + so quick to do. At 3.p.m. we went to "A" Battery finishing it at 4.p.m. in all 300 horses were tested, work ended out be continued owing to the light failing. Met the A.D.V.S. outside my billet who gave name & address + a few spare needles in case of accidents; a move of the Division is expected some say to Egypt. 9 am personally convinced of this, having my buildings just completed, + more have to move. What luck!	
	6th		Went to "B" Battery H'drs Bry continued testing. Had all horses turned round in stalls, 3 twitches & men to each, did 125 horses in 30 minutes.	

WAR DIARY
or
INTELLIGENCE SUMMARY.
(Erase heading not required.)

Army Form C. 2118.

Place	Date	Hour	Summary of Events and Information	Remarks and references to Appendices
Watin	6th		Found it better to tuberc all horses as one loses time, line where one a couple of horses. Went to "D" Battery finished it in 40 minutes. Some of the horses were standing in the open top to their knees in mud, this delayed me somewhat. Went to H.Q. of 2nd Bgde & finished the test of "A" + "C" Batteries. Examined in the afternoon — no reaction.	
	7th		Went to "B" + "D" Batteries + H.Q.s to examine the horses. Found one horse with his eye closed, examined him carefully, found a suppurating wound over the eye the result of a kick, otherwise nothing to be seen, except a small puffy swelling in lower eyelid. He resented the needle. In the afternoon went to the 4 & 5th Field Ambulance applied the test.	
	8th		Went to the 4 & 3rd Field Ambulance applied test, went to Chateau Couture to draw money to pay NCO's + men.	

(Stamp: 26th MOBILE VETERINARY SECTION)

WAR DIARY
INTELLIGENCE SUMMARY
(Erase heading not required.)

Army Form C. 2118.

Place	Date	Hour	Summary of Events and Information	Remarks and references to Appendices
Walton	8th		Visited 4th Field Ambulance. No readers. Paid MCB's a visit. No S.E 2809, Pte Smart R.R reports for duty from No 1 Vety Hospital.	
"	9th		Visited 4 & 2nd Field Ambulance. No readers.	
"	10th		Went to No 3 Section D.A.C to finish those not done by the V.O's a few days previously. The camp is on new ground, a good many mules & some horses are in the open, almost impossible to move round. 501 lines shifted, a good many were covered. In one instance the mule lines were in the hollow, standing up to the fetlock in liquid mud; pointed this out to O.C. who had them shifted onto high ground - muddy no doubt but not so bad. Saw the farrier sergeant. Drew young transferred to No 1 & Pte Train, Driver Musgrave taking his place. Examined No 3 Section D.A.C. No readers. Visited No 2 Section D.A.C & No 13 D.A.C.	
	11th		Those remaining + No 13. V.H. yesterday we are now examining those weekly Fridays + Mondays only, both large numbers of sick one there having very dry accommodation for twenty in any sick lines. No S.E 1232 & Pte Barnes W. reports from 2nd M.V.S. for duty. Twenty three horses evacuated to No 13 V.H.	

Army Form C. 2118.

WAR DIARY
or
INTELLIGENCE SUMMARY.
(Erase heading not required.)

Place	Date	Hour	Summary of Events and Information	Remarks and references to Appendices
Walon	12th		Entrained No 2. Section D.A.C. Advce to. No reactors. Corrugation removed from roof of sick lines as I could not get 18 sheets more to complete same; but the oilcloth was used to table, putting the	
"	13th		completely two animals evacuated to page to day. Twenty more sent up the hub for the new. Saddle + rifle inspection. Routine as usual. S.S. Judd proceeds to England on leave.	
"	14th		Routine as usual. Have arranged for a S. Smith to attend section for one hour daily from No 2. Co. Div Train. Kit inspection held.	
"	15d		A lot of sick horses in section about forty in number, very busy. Routine as usual. Send in of application for leave to A.D.V.S.	
"	16.		More sick horses arrive. Have two ambulances told very busy.	
"	17th		Sixty two horses sent to the base; ninet wagons, this leaves me about 4 men to carry on in the section, can do nothing but watch.	
"	18th		Feed the horses remaining in Section.	
"			More sick horses arrive, am at my wits end for men, the cannot	

WAR DIARY
or
INTELLIGENCE SUMMARY

Army Form C. 2118.

Place	Date	Hour	Summary of Events and Information	Remarks and references to Appendices
Walm.	19th		Lost for long. A.F.B. 213. rendered duty, also progress report on wagons, ammunition, clothing etc. Lieut. Carroll V.O. 1/c. 49th Brig. R.F.A. takes over command of the Section, as I am proceeding on leave to-morrow.	
	20th		My Corporal in course back from the Base Hospital reports that 6 of my men are under arrest for refusing to obey an order at the Hospital. As I am going on leave, I wire the A.D.V.S. reports same, + leaving the matter entirely in his hands. Proceeded on leave.	
"	27th		S.S. Judd now a farrier Sergt. transferred to No. 6 Vety. Hospital.	
"	28th		I arrive back from leave, having been wired for, as the Division is ordered to move. On arrival I found all movement orders cancelled. S.S. Mitchell from No. 6 Vety. Hospital reports for duty. A/MQ5026 Pte. Lannin J. reports for duty from No. 19 Vety. Hospital. Routine as usual. Saddle rifle inspection.	
"	29th			
"	30th		Collected 4 horses belonging to 9th Division near Steenwoorde. (one ambulance case)	

Army Form C. 2118.

WAR DIARY
or
INTELLIGENCE SUMMARY.
(Erase heading not required.)

Instructions regarding War Diaries and Intelligence Summaries are contained in F. S. Regs., Part II. and the Staff Manual respectively. Title pages will be prepared in manuscript.

Place	Date	Hour	Summary of Events and Information	Remarks and references to Appendices
Sabis	31st		Twenty two horses evacuated to No 13 V.H. Routine as usual.	F.J. Weir Capt. A.V.C. O.C. 26 M.V.S.

26th MOBILE VETERINARY SECTION [stamp]

Army Form C. 2118.

Instructions regarding War Diaries and Intelligence
Summaries are contained in F.S. Regs., Part II.
and the Staff Manual respectively. Title pages
will be prepared in manuscript.

WAR DIARY
or
INTELLIGENCE SUMMARY.
(Erase heading not required.)

Place	Date	Hour	Summary of Events and Information	Remarks and references to Appendices
WATOU	1st Jan		Evacuated 2 h horses to the base from Poperinghe.	
"	2nd		Routine as usual. Sent an orderly to Poperinghe for wagon.	
"	3rd		Visit by A.D.V.S. Routine as usual. Sent four more cases to the Base.	
"	4th		Routine as usual. Visit 6th Corps H.Q. at CHATEAU LOWE. Drew money for NCOs & men. Visit 6th Corps 1st Q. Sent ambulance horses & horse of the 4/5 Dn North of Poperinghe.	
"	5th		Saddle & rifle inspection. Visit 6th & Corp 1st Q. Went to WORMHOUDT to collect a horse belonging to another division, with my ambulance.	
"	6th		Routine as usual.	
"	7th		Sent an orderly to Crontre for wagon.	
"	8th		Sent twelve sick animals to the Base. Two helmet inspection held.	
"	9th		Routine as usual. Three more sick horses undergoing treatment in the section.	
"	10th		Routine as usual.	
"	11th		Saddle rifle inspection. Routine as usual.	

WAR DIARY or INTELLIGENCE SUMMARY

Army Form C. 2118.

Place	Date	Hour	Summary of Events and Information	Remarks and references to Appendices
WATOU	12th		Sent an orderly to GODEVAERVELDE for wagons. Sent to POPERINGHE for coal.	
"	13th		Evacuated 24 horses to the base.	
"	14th		Routine as usual. Sent to Godewaersvelde for wagons	
"	15th		Evacuated 29 Animals to the base. Sent to ABELE for saw dust for stables.	
"	16th		Saddle & rifle inspection. Went round 46 Bde. R.F.A.	
"	17th		Took over charge of 4 & 6 Bde R.F.A. Went to Hechingut & horses between Q.W. Train & 49th Div D.A.C.	
"	18th		Spent morning cutting manure had foot cases, cutting away the whole of the sole. Sick line stable floor thoroughly cleaned out. Officer on a horse with a very bad wound in the rectum. At 10 p.m. went to B Baty 46th Bde R.F.A. & shot a horse with fracture of the result of a kick.	
"	19th		Went to 46 Bde. Routine as usual. Went 42nd Field Ambulance.	
"	20th		Sent in charge of the 6 Corps HQ with Major to the base. Went to 46th Field Ambulance. Sgt. Campbell was placed under arrest for being drunk in charge of a wagon.	

WAR DIARY or INTELLIGENCE SUMMARY

Place	Date	Hour	Summary of Events and Information	Remarks and references to Appendices
Watou	21st	—	Sent to the base 2 & 2 sick animals.	
— " —	22nd	—	Saddle + rifle inspection. Visit by A.D.V.S. Sgt. Campbell brought Major Bartlett who put him back to a cart practice.	
— " —	23rd	—	Three NCO's new Officers having visited the B.D. visit. Orders received from H.Q. re times of Sgt. Campbell to be told off 2, 4 & 2 mob.	
— " —	24th	—	Proceeded to H.Q. with Sgt. Roberts, Cpl. Hughes, Pte. Childers & Sgt. Campbell the final war finished after an hour's duration. Took khaki inspection.	
— " —	25th	—	Sent to Godewaersvelde for wagons.	
— " —	26th	—	Sent to base 15 fourteen animals. Received the names of the erstwhile of Sgt. Campbell. he is to be reduced to the ranks, having 4, 2 days F.P. No1 remitted by the confirming officer. The whole section paraded, the sentence read out, and confirmed.	
— " —	27th	—		
— " —	28th	—	Sent 28 animals to the base. Went to conference at A.D.V.S.'s Office Vlamertinghe. It is proposed to have a central point for collection of sick horses. Poperinghe is the place decided on, where the animals will be handed over to me for entraining. This is owing to the distance between the units & the Motor Section, the Division being around North of Ypres.	

Army Form C. 2118.

WAR DIARY
or
INTELLIGENCE SUMMARY.
(Erase heading not required.)

Instructions regarding War Diaries and Intelligence Summaries are contained in F.S. Regs., Part II. and the Staff Manual respectively. Title pages will be prepared in manuscript.

Place	Date	Hour	Summary of Events and Information	Remarks and references to Appendices
Natu	29th		Saddle rifle inspection. Routine as usual.	
—	30th		Routine as usual.	
—	31st		Paid NCO's + men. Routine as usual.	

J. Weir.
F. Baker A.V.C.
O.C.

14

26.th Inch: Peh: Seer

Vol: 9

Army Form C. 2118.

WAR DIARY
or
INTELLIGENCE SUMMARY.
(Erase heading not required.)

Instructions regarding War Diaries and Intelligence Summaries are contained in F.S. Regs., Part II. and the Staff Manual respectively. Title pages will be prepared in manuscript.

Place	Date	Hour	Summary of Events and Information	Remarks and references to Appendices
~~Beauvois~~ WATOU.	Feb 1st		Nineteen sick horses sent to the Base from GODEWAERSVELDE	
— " —	2nd		Sent ambulance to 6th Corps H.Q. to fetch a horse belonging to Maj. Ingram suffering from congestion of the lungs.	
— " —	3rd		Went to POPERINGHE Station as arranged by A.D.V.S. brought eighty sick horses with me (two in the ambulance). On arrival there forty six animals were waiting, gave receipts, wrote labels, descriptive rolls etc. Fortunately the day was fine, otherwise I would have had great difficulty in writing the various documents I think on occasions like this, it would be better if the descriptive rolls were written by the V.O's. If the units concerned, then they could be ready except I strained hay for the horses from another division who were unloading hay at this station.	
— " —	4d		Received 24 sick horses. sent an orderly to Poperinghe for wagons. Routine as usual.	

WAR DIARY
or
INTELLIGENCE SUMMARY.

Army Form C. 2118.

Place	Date	Hour	Summary of Events and Information	Remarks and references to Appendices
WATOU.	5th		Entrained horses at POPERINGHE for the Base.	
"	6th		Routine as usual.	
"	7th		Sent 35 sick animals to the Base.	
"	8th		Sent orderly to POPERINGHE for orders.	
"	9th		Met A.D.V.S. at Poperinghe, who brought me in a motor car to see new billets as we are going to move out of this district. Sent 24 Animals to the Base.	
"	10th		Inspection of smoke helmets. Routine as usual.	
"	11th		Ordered weighing at Poperinghe. Received orders to move out on Monday 14th inst.	

WAR DIARY
INTELLIGENCE SUMMARY

Place	Date	Hour	Summary of Events and Information	Remarks and references to Appendices
WATOU	12th		Sent 24 sick horses to the Base from Poperinghe.	
"	13th		Sent a billeting party to take over new billets from 32nd M.V.S. Saddle rifle inspection.	
"	14th		Left Watou for new billets between WORMHOUDT and LEDRINGHEM. Got out after a struggle at 12 noon, one gets so miserable after 4 months in the one place. I am sorry to leave my stables still I have had good value out of them, but certainly all are glad to leave Belgium; they are so mean, they won't always their fund of feed. Left few sick horses for the 32nd M.V.S. West via WINNIZEELE where we halted for ½ hour. Arrived at WORMHOUDT at 3.30 p.m. got to billets at 4.30 p.m. they are good billets. An estate there for horses with plenty of straw	

WAR DIARY
or
INTELLIGENCE SUMMARY.
(Erase heading not required.)

Army Form C. 2118.

Place	Date	Hour	Summary of Events and Information	Remarks and references to Appendices
LEDRINGHEM	16th		All the horses are in barns; the people here are most amiable. Got wagons untoward, flag & direction posts in position, horse property tried up & another line for sewing cleanside. Got billets thoroughly cleaned out.	
"	17th		Have a fair number foiets horses to keep all busy. Visit by A.D.V.S.	
"	18th		Went to SEINE HOUCK to collect a horse left by the 49th Div. It had died, gave a certificate of death from the mayor at ARNEKE. Visit by A.D.V.S, held a saddle & rifle inspection. Entrained twenty one sick horses at ARNEKE. Visited by the A.D.V.S. & Col Chandler reported sick & sent to 51st Field Ambulance.	
"	19th		Eleven remounts brought here lying men from ARNEKE for distribution	

WAR DIARY
or
INTELLIGENCE SUMMARY
(Erase heading not required.)

Army Form C. 2118.

Place	Date	Hour	Summary of Events and Information	Remarks and references to Appendices
Watun	20th		Distributed remounts to their units. Sent one man away by train from ESQUELBECQ somewhere South — I believe AMIENS — as billeting party.	
	21st		Sent seven sick horses to the base from Arneke. Had to evacuate one of my best ponies to the base, as he was unable to walk, the result of a suppurating wound in his fetlock. Received orders to proceed to CASSEL on the 22nd inst. Two days rations being carried in my supply wagon. Reveille to-morrow morning at 2 a.m.	
	22.		Marched into H. a.m. Quartz. Van huns's hall at Zu Typpen* to entrain horses. Arriving at BAVINGHOVE at 7.30 a.m. Started entraining at 8 a.m. wagons were loaded first, was entrained by 9 a.m. Left CASSEL at 10.30 a.m. with the D.L.O.Y. + Cable Section R.E. Arrived at AMIENS at 8 p.m. where I was told to pick up one charger in my ambulance which was injured during railway journey earlier in the day. Received orders from the D.A. + Q.M.G. to proceed to St VAAST EN CHAUSSÉE. Also a map of AMIENS, where I arrived at 3 a.m. Men were placed in	

WAR DIARY
or
INTELLIGENCE SUMMARY.

Army Form C. 2118.

Place	Date	Hour	Summary of Events and Information	Remarks and references to Appendices
ST VAAST EN CHAUSSE	23rd		Good billets, + the horses were all under cover.	
	24th		Had great difficulty in obtaining rations, everything of supplies was absolutely upset. Inspection of tube helmets.	
			Orders arrived at 4 a.m. to move at 9 a.m. under the D.A.C. to BEAUVAL. Received two mules over from B/49 R.F.A. Billeting party sent on ahead to arrange billets. Stayed the horses at BERTANGLES wherever watered & fed the horses. Reached BEAUVAL at 7 p.m. Had good stabling for the horses, and a good billets for the men & myself.	
BEAUVAL	25th		Received two horses from 2/D.A.C. two from 43 Bde M.G.Co. Got orders to proceed to ETREE WAMIN. via DOULLENS under the D.A.C. Sent horses & the ambulance to CANDAS. Snow was falling, and marching was rendered very difficult, could get no further than DOULLENS that night. Decided to billet here. The C.O of the casualty clearing station was good enough to place a large hut at our disposal. Horses were picketed along	

Army Form C. 2118.

WAR DIARY
or
INTELLIGENCE SUMMARY.
(Erase heading not required.)

Instructions regarding War Diaries and Intelligence Summaries are contained in F. S. Regs., Part II. and the Staff Manual respectively. Title pages will be prepared in manuscript.

Place	Date	Hour	Summary of Events and Information	Remarks and references to Appendices
DOULLENS	26th		The Boulevarde in the snow with rugs on. Ambulance has not arrived yet. Sent two horses back for my ambulance as I was told it was usable to get up the hills from BEAUVAL, the roads being so slippery. Proceeded to ETREE WAMIN, started at 12.noon. Roads were still bad. Proceeded dismounted. Arrived at new billets at 6.30 p.m. Horses under cover, men in a good barn.	
ETRÉE WAMIN.	27th		Received five sick horses. Saddle & rifle inspection.	
	28th		Received few sick animals, got orders to proceed to LIGNEREUIL. Sent all sick to FRÉVENT, nine in all, with two dismounted men. No billets available, so found good places for men + horses at BLAVINCOURT.	
BLAVINCOURT	29		Received one case of Pneumonia from Div. Train. J. W. R. Bapista	

WAR DIARY
or
INTELLIGENCE SUMMARY.
(Erase heading not required.)

Army Form C. 2118.

Place	Date	Hour	Summary of Events and Information	Remarks and references to Appendices
BLAVINCOURT	March 2nd 12th		Visit by A.D.V.S. Received orders to proceed to BARLEY to-morrow the 2nd unit starts from midday (LAHERLIÈRE). Saddle miles inspection held which is not very far from midday.	
BARLY	2nd		Marched out at 10.a.m. to BARLEY, about 6 miles distance. Arrived at 12. noon. Got one large haystack cleared for section horses. The sick lines are in barns in Rue D'AVESNES. Billets not very good for men, as they are situated in three different places.	
	3rd		Got sick lines put in order, also section lines. Went to H.Q at BERNEVILLE to draw pay for NCO's & men.	
	4th		Sent an orderly to railhead 15 under waggons for sick horses. Routine as usual.	
	5th		Sent 7 sick horses to the base. D.R.E.M.S. MARSHELL transferred to No 16 A. Sec.	

Army Form C. 2118.

WAR DIARY
or
INTELLIGENCE SUMMARY.
(Erase heading not required.)

Instructions regarding War Diaries and Intelligence Summaries are contained in F.S. Regs., Part II. and the Staff Manual respectively. Title pages will be prepared in manuscript.

[Stamp: 5th MOBILE VETERINARY SECTION]

Place	Date	Hour	Summary of Events and Information	Remarks and references to Appendices
BARLY	5th		M. ARCHAMBAUD. Junr Section as in Corporale. D.V. TOVEY joins Section from No.1 Co. A.S.C.	
"	6th		Went to rail head, to meet remounts; these did not arrive until 11.5.p.m. Horses were allotted to the various units in the wagons, as owing to endless confusion in the darkness. Saddle up the inspection held. Routine as usual.	
"	7th			
"	8th		Smoke helmet inspection held. Routine as usual.	
"	9th		Took over charge of 43rd Field ambulance wagons ordered for Base to remount.	
"	10th		Went to LINGHEREIL. to visit 43rd Fd. Amb. Went on to SARS LES BOIS to arrange about collection of horse left by 4th Brig. R.F.A. with a Wound Punch (picked up on rd) 22 sick horses sent to the Base.	

1577 [Wt. W10791/773 500,000 1/15 D.D. & L. A.D.S.S./Forms/C. 2118.

WAR DIARY
or
INTELLIGENCE SUMMARY

Army Form C. 2118.

Place	Date	Hour	Summary of Events and Information	Remarks and references to Appendices
BARLY	11th		Sent ambulance to SARS, LES BOIS for horse, it is being kept for treatment to re-issue to its own unit again (49 Bry R.F.A.) Parcel of comforts received from A.V.C. Fund.	
"	12th		Three horses dropped in town by fire, brown carthorses, no damage done. Went to Sus St LEGER to arrange about collection of horses left by 61st Co. R.E. this horse is fit to walk, & no use sent an orderly to - mornin for him.	
"	13th		Horse collected. Troops ordered for leave. Routine as usual.	
"	14th		Rifle saddle & smoke helmet inspection. 15 horses sent to the Base.	
"	15th		Took over charge of 49th Brig + Cav Squadron at FOSSEUX during Lt MEEKE'S absence on leave.	
"	16th		Lt Thomas junr Section to replace Lt Marshall who has been transferred to No 1 Co. A.S.C. Troops ordered for the Base.	

WAR DIARY
or
INTELLIGENCE SUMMARY.
(Erase heading not required.)

Army Form C. 2118.

Place	Date	Hour	Summary of Events and Information	Remarks and references to Appendices
BARLY.	17th		Visited 49th Bgde R.F.A. + Cavalry Squadron. munition to the Base.	
	18th		Received orders to proceed to FOSSEUX as BARLY is no longer in our area, on the 19th inst. No new billets are only 1 Kilometre away; I went out and saw the Town Commandant who showed me my new billets, which are very good for men + horses. The sick lines are about 200 yards away, a disadvantage.	
FOSSEUX.	19th		Proceeded to FOSSEUX; brought a few sick horses with me + one in the ambulance. Sent for straw to GRAND ROULECOURT as no straw is available in this town, for the men.	
	20th		Visit 49/R.F.A. + Cav. Squadron. Pte. ASHWORTH proceeds on leave. Trucks ordered for the Base.	

WAR DIARY
or
INTELLIGENCE SUMMARY.

Place	Date	Hour	Summary of Events and Information	Remarks and references to Appendices
FOSSEUX	22nd		Rifle, saddle & water helmet inspection. Visit by A.D.V.S. Went to 43rd Fd. Amb. LINGUEREL. Fifteen horses evacuated to the Base.	
"			Visit 49 R.F.A & Cav. Squadron, held p.m. in a horse & cattle unit made a careful search for the anneal forage put in the American rickes. 9 cats. negative result. Two of these forage have been found in 46/R.F.A, they were sent to 5 Div. H.Q. For examination. All vats are now spread out in a large tarpaulin, and carefully examined before use. Pte IMPEY reports for duty from No. 6. Vety Hospital.	
"	23rd		Visit 49th Brig R.F.A. at WANQUENTIN. Met A.D.V.S. there; held an inspection of the B. echs. Tracks ordered for the B echs of the animals.	

WAR DIARY
or
INTELLIGENCE SUMMARY.

(Erase heading not required.)

Army Form C. 2118.

Place	Date	Hour	Summary of Events and Information	Remarks and references to Appendices
FOSSEUX.	24d.		Visited Cav. Squadron. 13 sick animals evacuated to the Base.	
—,, —	25d.		Visited 49th Bde. at WANQUETIN. also 47th Brig. R.F.A. & Div. Cavalry. Routine as usual.	
—,, —	26d.		Saddle & rifle inspection held. Visited Div. Cavalry. 47th Bde. R.F.A. Ordered trucks for Base.	
—,, —	27d.		Twelve horses evacuated. Went to WANQUENTIN to meet up 47/R.F.A. Went up A.D.V.S. Pte ADAMS & Pte THOMPSON posted on leave. Horses picketed in the open, weather splendid.	
—,, —	28d.		Routine as usual.	
—,, —	29d.		Trucks ordered for Base. Farm cleaned up visit in & fitting stable after the French.	
—,, —	30d.		Visit Cavalry squadron. 10 horses evacuated. Handed over the 49th Brig. R.F.A. to Capt CARROLL & Capt MEEK & his returns from leave.	
—,, —	31d.			

J.J.W...
Capt...
O.C.

26 M vers
vol 10

WAR DIARY
or
INTELLIGENCE SUMMARY
(Erase heading not required.)

Army Form C. 2118.

26 Mvs
Vol II

Place	Date	Hour	Summary of Events and Information	Remarks and references to Appendices
FOSSEUX	April 2nd		Ten horses evacuated to the Base. Visit by A.D.V.S. Went to Cavalry Squadron. Sgt to ABBEVILLE for a R.S.P.C.A. Ambulance, one limber wagon returned in lieu.	
"	April 3rd		A.D.V.S. proceeds on leave, took over his duties during his absence. Routine as usual.	
"	3rd		Went to H.Q. 14 Division. Visit Cavalry Squadron. I am at present very busy, W/F by the French, being carried away somewhere, met the remt. of air men of the Dis. Agilash	
"	4th		Went to the H.Q. Saddlers. Saddle rifle inspection also fair inspection. Routine as usual. Ambulance arrives from ABBEVILLE. I have made two runs out & got in BELGIUM – four wheeler – carries two horses in much better than the first arrived.	
"	5th		Went to Div. H.Q. Routine as usual.	
"	6th		Visit Cavalry Squadron. Surrounded by Wagons to SAILLY.	
"	7th		Went to Div. H.Q. Seven horses mange cases Trimmed. Sup[?] in Ammunition evacuated to the Base.	

WAR DIARY
or
INTELLIGENCE SUMMARY

Army Form C. 2118.

26th MOB. 1st ARMY VETERINARY SECTION

Place	Date	Hour	Summary of Events and Information	Remarks and references to Appendices
FOSSEUX	8th		Went to Div. H.Q. Held a P.M. of the cavalry squadron. Routine as usual.	
"	9th		Held helmet inspected. Went to Div. H.Q.	
"	10th		Went to Div. H.Q. Visit cavalry squadron. Routine as usual. Sent for wagons to Saulty.	
"	11th		Nine horses evacuated to the Base. Routine as usual.	
"	12th		Went to Div. A.D. Saddle + rifle inspection held.	
"	13th		Routine as usual.	
"	14th		A.D.V.S. returns from leave. Sent to Saulty for wagons. Paid N.C.O's + men.	
"	15th		Visit by A.D.V.S. & in lorry visits the hills. Unfortunately most of the men & horses were away at Saulty evacuating horses, as the horses are looking well.	
"	16th		Routine as usual.	
"	17th		Took over duty charge of the D.A.C., they are in very poor condition, and at the present time are in this fletcher in mud. Head horses lines moved onto hard ground.	
"	18th		Inspection of D.A.C. by A.D.V.S. 24 horses picked out + placed on a separate	

WAR DIARY
INTELLIGENCE SUMMARY

(Erase heading not required.)

Army Form C. 2118.

[Stamp: N° 26th MOBILE VETERINARY SECTION]

Place	Date	Hour	Summary of Events and Information	Remarks and references to Appendices
FOSSEUX	18th		Line, as they were in very poor condition. Scrapings were taken from the few of them & sent to the Mobile Lab. 4th 3rd Fl. Amb. for examination no microsp. has arrived yet for the M.V.S. Result. Negative for mange. Calcium Sulphide dressing has been used, & a good many of these horses are getting their hair again, they being practically have worked necks & body.	
	19th-		Inspection of saddlery &c. SE No 676. Pte Wilson W. reports for duty from No. 2 Vety Hospital HAVRE. I am now one surplus, why he was sent here I cannot say, we did our return show one short in the previous AFB 2113. Went to DAO Sent to SAULTY for wagons.	
	20th-		Thirty two horses sent to the Base. Went to DAC. Visit by ADVS	
	21st-		Routine as usual. Went to DAC.	
	22nd-		Went to DAC. Routine as usual.	
	23rd-		Inspection of Tube Helmets. Sent to SAULTY for wagons.	

Army Form C. 2118.

WAR DIARY
or
INTELLIGENCE SUMMARY
(Erase heading not required.)

Instructions regarding War Diaries and Intelligence Summaries are contained in F.S. Regs., Part II. and the Staff Manual respectively. Title Pages will be prepared in manuscript.

Place	Date	Hour	Summary of Events and Information	Remarks and references to Appendices
FOSSEUX	24th		Sixteen horses sent to the Base. Visit D.A.C.	
"	25th		Routine as usual. Visit Cavalry Squadron.	
"	26th		Sent b/Sadly. for negro. Visit D.A.C. Rifle + saddle inspection held.	
"	27th		Twenty one animals sent to the Base. Visit D.A.C.	
"	28th		Routine as usual. Visit Cavalry Squadron. Visit by A.D.V.S.	
"	29th		Visit D.A.C. routine as usual.	
"	30th		Routine as usual. Visit by A.D.V.S.	

F. Gwilim
Capt. A.V.C.
O.C. 26th Mobile Veterinary Section

Army Form C. 2118.

vol 12
XIV
26 M.V.S.

WAR DIARY
or
INTELLIGENCE SUMMARY

(Erase heading not required.)

Instructions regarding War Diaries and Intelligence Summaries are contained in F.S. Regs., Part II. and the Staff Manual respectively. Title Pages will be prepared in manuscript.

Place	Date	Hour	Summary of Events and Information	Remarks and references to Appendices
Fosseux	May 1st	—	23 Sick animals evacuated to the Base. S.S. Mitchell & 14 men proceeded on leave	
"	2nd	—	Saddle and Rifle inspection made by the A.D.V.S. Routine as usual & sick	
"	3rd	—	Sent to duty to order horses for hospital.	
"	4	—	14 Sick animals sent to the Base. Lieut Melville proc. to new Billets. Lieut Neumann proc. to our Alegar to Base	
Helaincamp	5th	—	16. Animals sent to the Base. Left Fosseux proceeded to H.Q.t Hlaincamp from H.Q. & men to order horses	
"	6th	—	Visited by the A.D.V.S. Sent to South Foudri Bois Bethune, 2½ chlometros to take horses to Valoi	
"	7th	—	4 Animals evacuated to Base. Routine as usual	
"	8th	—	Sent 12 orderlys to order horses. Methods use own tents arrived for use of Lector Thoroughly arrived for use of Lector	
"	9th	—	8 Animals evacuated to the Base. Visited by the A.D.V.S. Rifles and use of Hemel emphasised Rd. orders transferred from this Lector. Lt. N.Q. Wys Reg sp Lab	
"	10th	—	Sent to Longues to order horses for the Base LaVele inspection Routine as usual	
"	11th	—	40 Animals evacuated to the Base. Evacuation of the A.D.V.S. demo out of the storm sick went to fetch horses and Germen men. 9th P.V.B. 116 8 men	
"	12th	—	Routine as usual visited by the A.D.V.S. 9th P.V.B. Sec 116 V.B.O. 8 men	
"	13th	—	Sent to Longues to order horses for the Base. The Departure of the Interpreter	
"	14th	—	14 Animals evacuated to the Base. Routine as usual	

J. Whisbery
for Major

Army Form C. 2118.

WAR DIARY
or
INTELLIGENCE SUMMARY

(Erase heading not required.)

Instructions regarding War Diaries and Intelligence Summaries are contained in F. S. Regs., Part II. and the Staff Manual respectively. Title Pages will be prepared in manuscript.

Place	Date	Hour	Summary of Events and Information	Remarks and references to Appendices
Hesdin	15th	—	Vet inspection. Arrival of another Interpreter. Visit to the A.D.V.S. Horse Ambs. as usual. Sent to stubbing to Dr. Wagris.	
—	16th	—	Saddle & Rifle inspection. Nine animals evacuated to the Base. Routine as usual.	
—	17th	—	Sent to stubbing to order boxes for the Base. R.S.P. Cat. Spray ordered for use of Section.	
—	18th	—	Twelve animals evacuated to the Base. Routine as usual.	
—	19th	—	Visited the A.D.V.S. Sent to Doumelle to R.E. Horse. Coll. Weir met with an accident, fractured his nose an animal devoured into hospital.	
—	20th	—	Capt. Brown V.O. of the 47th Bgde takes charge of the Section and visits the 47th Bgde R.F.A & 142 Inf Bgde	
—	21st	—	Visits to A.D.V.S. Sent to stubbing to order Boxes for the Base.	
—	22nd	—	Twenty animals evacuated to the Base. Visit to the 47th Bgde R.F.A. The driver Pte Stubbs proceeded on leave. Visit to the A.D.V.S. Routine as usual.	
—	23rd	—	Visited 47th Bgde R.F.A. P.M.E. on one horse. Rifle & Sadd inspection. Routine as usual. Cable and Ambulance	
—	24th	—	Visit to 42" Divs Ambulance and 47" Bgde R.F.A. Sent to stubbing to order boxes and Ambulance to the D.A.D.S. for one horse sent Ambulance to Doumelle for one horse. Routine as usual.	
—	25th	—	Seventeen animals evacuated to the Base. Pte Groves met with an accident and admitted into hospital.	
—	26th	—	Visit to the A.D.V.S. Routine as usual.	

[Stamp: 5th MOBILE VETERINARY SECTION No. 9 Date 21-3-16]

Army Form C. 2118.

WAR DIARY
or
INTELLIGENCE SUMMARY
(Erase heading not required.)

Instructions regarding War Diaries and Intelligence Summaries are contained in F.S. Regs., Part II. and the Staff Manual respectively. Title Pages will be prepared in manuscript.

Place	Date	Hour	Summary of Events and Information	Remarks and references to Appendices
Telegraph	27	—	Visits by A.D.V.S. & D.D.V.S. went to fitt cashic and Gens conf for the men & Parr of N.C.O. & men	
—	28	—	Visits of the A.D.V.S. Sent to studly by 15 airdon Wagons for the Base Routine as usual	
—	29	—	Visits of the A.D.V.S. Evacuated seventeen animals to the Base	
—	30	—	Visits by the A.D.V.S. Routine as usual N° 3169 Colombo E.A. which to this section for Inj. from N° 6 vety Hospital Rouen	
—	31	—	Visits by the A.D.V.S. Routine as usual	

[Stamp: 26th MOBILE VETERINARY SECTION No. 3 Date 31-5-16]

2449 Wt. W14957/M90 750,000 1/16 J.B.C. & A. Forms/C.2118/12.

Army Form C. 2118.

Vol 13 June

WAR DIARY
or
INTELLIGENCE SUMMARY

(Erase heading not required.)

[Stamp: 26th MOBILE VETERINARY SECTION]

Place	Date	Hour	Summary of Events and Information	Remarks and references to Appendices
St Aubigny Farm	June 1st		Seven horses evacuated to No 22 Veterinary Hospital.	
	2nd		Capt J. Weir returned to section from No 1 Red Cross Hospital.	
	3rd		P.C. 20 th Medical Mobile Laboratory visited the section and drew blood from horses for serum.	
	4th		A.D.V.S. visited section. Ordered boxes at (Aubigny) AUBIGNY. Pte R.C. Rivers reported for duty with section as clerk.	
	5th		Ten horses evacuated from AUBIGNY to No 22 Vety Hospital. Capt J. M. Crow evacuated to No 2 Red Cross Hospital from 37th C.C.S. Services of a saddler from the R.A.S.C. were enlisted to repair harness.	
		6 pm	Horse ambulance sent to DAINVILLE.	
	6th		Visit by A.D.M.S. Sanitary arrangements of camp approved. Wounded war horse suffering from wounds gunshot (shrapnel) Horses were moved into stables on account of inclemency of weather. Repairs carried out on farm forge and on ambulance	

WAR DIARY or INTELLIGENCE SUMMARY

Army Form C. 2118.

Place	Date	Hour	Summary of Events and Information	Remarks and references to Appendices
Ste Scamps Siene	June 7th		I proceeded to MANIN to attend a case of colic (charger of 17th Batty R.G.A) Died P.M. Acute peritonitis due to rupture of stomach.	
	8th		Visit by A.D.V.S and Camp Commandant. A.D.V.S. ordered a parade of men and horses for Mon June 12th at 10.30 a.m. Monsieur Didier, interpreter, left section to join French Mission at 1st Div'l HQrs. Score boxes ordered at AUBIGNY.	
	9th		Fifty eight tube helmets were inspected. Said N.C.O's & men 555 francs. Seven horses evacuated to No.22 Vet Hosp. from AUBIGNY. Army canteen was started in the section.	
	10th		Ambulance wheel sent to Divl Ammn Sub Park to be re-bushed by permission of Lieut. 90 workshops.	
	11th		Inspection of kit, rifles & saddlery and veterinary equipment.	
	12th		A.D.V.S inspected the unit in full marching order. In the test turn out, mounted, 15 fcs were awarded to Pte. W.Beverly (cont'd)	790

WAR DIARY
or
INTELLIGENCE SUMMARY

Army Form C. 2118.

Place	Date	Hour	Summary of Events and Information	Remarks and references to Appendices
Hillocamp Farm	June 12th		2nd Wing 10/c awarded to Pte R R Smart. Pte R Bifford received Wing for bed turned out wagon. Pte H.E. Franklin proceeded on leave to England. A colt belonging to the farmer was castrated and docked. Sent to AUBIGNY for boxes. Went to WAN QUETIN to examine horses of No 4 Coy A.S.C. Tested with mallein for Glanders.	
	13th		Five animals evacuated to No 22nd Vety Hospital. Purchased a small barrel from farmer for fomentations.	
	14th		Pte J. E. Carton & P. Kelly transferred to No 2 Veterinary Hospital in accordance with A.B.v.S. memo No 213/13 Y. of 11th inst. Daylight Saving came into force.	
	15th		Stores drawn from D.A.D.V.S. Destroyed two horses. Post mortem examination held.	
	16th		Lieut. J. L. Clark reported for duty with 47th R.F.A. A.D.V.S. visited the section.	
	17th		Ambulance wheel returned from Divl Ammn Sub Park	

WAR DIARY or INTELLIGENCE SUMMARY

(Erase heading not required.)

Army Form C. 2118.

Place	Date	Hour	Summary of Events and Information	Remarks and references to Appendices
Aubigny Farm	18th		Horse trucks ordered at AUBIGNY.	
	19th		Lorries for watering of horses at LATTRE ST QUENTIN altered to 7.0 a.m. 12.0 noon and 5.30 p.m. 13 horses evacuated to No 22 Vetty Hospital Cover for horse ambulance received from J.H. Gilson Bay TUNBRIDGE WELLS.	
	20th		A.D.V.S. visited the section.	
	21st		Requested O.C. No 22 Vet Hospital to relieve men taking horses to ABBEVILLE at an earlier hour, in order that they are not compelled to wait 24 hrs for return train.	
	22nd		I left section to proceed on leave to IRELAND from June 23rd to July 1st Lieut J.R. Clark assumed charge of the section. Three trucks ordered at AUBIGNY.	
	23rd		12 horses and one mule evacuated from AUBIGNY to No 22 Vet Hospital. N.C.O's and men had 6.0 francs.	
	24th		On return of Pte H.E. Franklin from leave reported to A.D.V.S. Inspection of tube helmets	AJW

Army Form C. 2118.

WAR DIARY
or
INTELLIGENCE SUMMARY
(Erase heading not required.)

Instructions regarding War Diaries and Intelligence Summaries are contained in F.S. Regs., Part II. and the Staff Manual respectively. Title Pages will be prepared in manuscript.

Place	Date	Hour	Summary of Events and Information	Remarks and references to Appendices
Hilversum/France	June 25th		Pte. P.H.Lloyd reported sick – excused duty. A.D.V.S. visited the section.	
	26th		Pte. P.H.Lloyd admitted to 24th Field Ambulance. A.D.V.S. visited the section. Inquiries made of O/C 200 Reserve (Home & Base) anent non return of Pte A.C. Franklin from leave.	
	27th		A.D.V.S. visited section.	
	28th		Nine horses entrained at AUBIGNY	
	29th		Eight horses evacuated to No 22 Vety Hospital. Pte N.E. Franklin returned to section from leave of absence in England. Papers submitted by him forwarded to A.D.V.S. Pte. P.H.Lloyd returned to section from 24th Fd Ambulance.	
	30th		Horse ambulance sent to DUISANS to collect a mare found by 2nd Glamorgan R.E. Also sent to collect two horses from No 4 Sec 14th D.A.C.	

J.W.Weir Capt AVC
?M

Army Form C.2118.

WAR DIARY
or
INTELLIGENCE SUMMARY

(Erase heading not required.)

July
14
26 M.V.S
Vol 14

Place	Date	Hour	Summary of Events and Information	Remarks and references to Appendices
FILESCAMP FARM	July 1st		The A.D.M.S 14th Div. Lt. Col Pryme accompanied by A.D.V.S Capt Longridge, and O.C. 25th San. Sec. Capt Pyke visited Section and inspected the sanitary and culinary arrangements. They were found generally satisfactory but one or two minor improvements were suggested.	
	July 2nd		A.D.V.S inspected the section. A.O. i/c visited section and microscopically examined scrapings taken from horses under suspicion for Mange. 4 animals were received for evacuation from 5th M.V.S. which was leaving the neighbourhood. Three wounded horses of the French Gendarmerie were admitted to the Section. Trucks for evacuation of horses on the morrow ordered at AUBIGNY. I arrived at section after leave of absence to Scotland.	
	July 3rd		14 animals, together with 11 received from 5th M.V.S. evacuated to S.622 Veterinary Hospital. Inspected the rifles and saddlery of the unit.	
	July 4th		Visited WARLUS. being appointed to act as A.D.V.S during the absence of	

Army Form C. 2118.

WAR DIARY or INTELLIGENCE SUMMARY

(Erase heading not required.)

Place	Date	Hour	Summary of Events and Information	Remarks and references to Appendices
FILESCAMP FARM.	July 4th		Major E.B. Baskett who had proceeded on leave of absence to England.	
	July 5th		Capt Steele visited the section for the purpose of inspecting scrapings taken from a horse suspected of mange. The parasite was found. (No 4 Coy 14th Div Train.) Drew 525 fes from Field Cashier to pay N.C.O's & men	
	July 6th		Went to WARLUS. Paid N.C.O's and men of the section. Trucks ordered at AUBIGNY for the evacuation of horses.	
	July 7th		Evacuated nine horses and one mule to No 22 Veterinary Hospital from AUBIGNY. Went to XI Corps HdQrs and inspected animals of HdQrs, Corps Signals + Corps Police	
	July 8th		Went to AUBIGNY and distributed remounts for 14th Div. units received from A.D.R. Third Army. Went to A.D.V.S. office and despatched weekly returns. Drew ten agehorses for section	
	July 9th		Weekly inspection of rifles and anti-gas helmets. Inspected the anti-gas helmets of the section and found all in good order Lt. Gen Cooper, Lt. Col Hamilton and	

WAR DIARY or INTELLIGENCE SUMMARY

Army Form C. 2118.

Place	Date	Hour	Summary of Events and Information	Remarks and references to Appendices
FILESCAMP FARM.	July 9th contd		Capt Pryer, G.O.C., A.A.&Q.M.G, G.S.O 3 respectively of the 14th Division visited the Section and inspected the horse lines, harness etc. Trucks ordered at AUBIGNY for the evacuation of horses on the morrow. Reviewed the time table of the Section	
	July 10th		Evacuated 13 horses and one mule to No 22 Veterinary Hospital from AUBIGNY. Visited VI Corps. Went to Warlus in the afternoon. Inspected rifles, saddlery and horses of the unit. First day of new time table - worked satisfactorily	
	July 11th		Went to Warlus. Ordered truck at AUBIGNY for evacuation of horses in the morrow	
	July 12th		Evacuated seven horses to No 22 Veterinary Hospital from AUBIGNY	
	July 13th		Inspected animals of VI Corps	
	July 14th		A.D.V.S. visited the Section. A cinematograph entertainment kindly given by the Rev. Capt Leal attached to G.H.Q. C.L.S. was well attended	
	July 15th		Trucks ordered at AUBIGNY for evacuation of horses on the morrow	

Army Form C. 2118.

Instructions regarding War Diaries and Intelligence Summaries are contained in F.S. Regs., Part II. and the Staff Manual respectively. Title Pages will be prepared in manuscript.

WAR DIARY
— or —
INTELLIGENCE SUMMARY

(Erase heading not required.)

Place	Date	Hour	Summary of Events and Information	Remarks and references to Appendices
FILESCAMP FARM	July 16th		Major E.B. Bartlett visited Section. Evacuated 15 horses and two mules to No 22 Vet Hospital from AUBIGNY. Lights placed at AUBIGNY for the embarkation of horses and mules.	
	July 17th		Divine Service conducted by the Rev Capt Hale was well attended. Visited VI Corps HQrs and 16th Lancers Yeomanry as Veterinary Officer. Inspection of rifles and saddlery.	
	July 18th		Major E.B. Bartlett A.D.V.S. visited the section.	
	July 19th		Inspected animals of section.	
	July 20th		Major E.B. Bartlett visited the section. Received 10 horses from Workers Company for distribution as remounts and one horse for evacuation in accordance with instructions received from D.D.V.R. Third Army. Three trucks at AUBIGNY.	
	July 21st		Evacuated 13 horses to No 22 Veterinary Hospital from AUBIGNY. Issued horses to VI Corps. Paid N.C.O.s and men 610 francs.	

Army Form C. 2118.

WAR DIARY
INTELLIGENCE SUMMARY
(Erase heading not required.)

26th MOBILE VETERINARY SECTION

Place	Date	Hour	Summary of Events and Information	Remarks and references to Appendices
FILESCAMP FARM.	July 22nd		Inspected animals of II Corps HQrs & Signals. Obtained a trough from 15th Reserve Park for watering sick horses. Attended a sick cow belonging to an inhabitant, also a foal.	
	July 23rd		Ordered trucks from AVBIGNY for the evacuation of horses on the morrow. Divine Service conducted by the Rev. Capt. Seale.	
	July 24th		Evacuated seven horses and two mules from AVBIGNY to No 22 Veterinary Hospital. Visited II Corps. A Veterinary Officer has now been appointed to II Corps from No. Ray I relinquish veterinary charge of animals of II Corps. Inspection of rifle & saddlery Capt. G.S. Thornewill V.O. to 46th N.B.A. visited section to examine samplings for mange. Fortnightly inspection of gas helmets.	
	July 25th		Truck arrived from AVBIGNY for the evacuation of horses on the morrow. New oven constructed for the cookhouse.	
	July 26th		Five horses evacuated to No. 22 Veterinary Hospital from AVBIGNY. Major E.B. Bartlett visited section prior to his departure to take up his new appointment. He introduced Capt. Dalgleish who had arrived to relieve him.	

Army Form C. 2118.

WAR DIARY or INTELLIGENCE SUMMARY

(Erase heading not required.)

Place	Date	Hour	Summary of Events and Information	Remarks and references to Appendices
FILESCAMP FARM.	July 27th		A.D.V.S. visited Section. Trucks arrived from AUBIGNY for evacuation of horses. Inspection of bandoliers and ammunition.	
	July 28th		Lieut J.L. Clark this batman who had been billeted with Section left for GRAND RULLECOURT in accordance with instructions. Went to AVESNES LE CONTE to draw pay for NCOs & men. Evacuated 15 horses to No22 Veterinary Section from AUBIGNY.	
		9.30pm	Received orders to proceed to SUS ST LEGER on 29th and to clear of AVESNES LE CONTE by 10.0 a.m. Paid N.C.O.'s & men of the Section 595 francs. Mons F. DIDIER of French Mission joined Section as interpreter.	
	July 29th		Reveille at 4.0 a.m.; camp struck billets dismantled &c. Left FILESCAMP at 8.30 a.m. and arrived at AVESNES LE CONTE at 9.50 a.m. Ahalt was called & kilometre beyond horses &c were inspected and everything was found in good order. Arrived at SUS ST LEGER 11.30 a.m. The billeting party, the interpreter Mons Dizier & Pte Beasley, and was conducted to the site of the camp. The site was a good one in many respects, but nearest water supply was about 1 kilometres distant Capt McHarper was sent to MARLU ZEL for orders.	
SUS ST LEGER	July 30th		Instructions received from Air.D.H22 that operation orders would be transmitted to the Section from HQrs of the 3rd Inf. Bde to which sm newly should be attached. Orders were received at noon from Capt P. Nyegaan DAQMG for	

Army Form C. 2118.

WAR DIARY
or
INTELLIGENCE SUMMARY
(Erase heading not required.)

Instructions regarding War Diaries and Intelligence Summaries are contained in F.S. Regs., Part II. and the Staff Manual respectively. Title Pages will be prepared in manuscript.

Place	Date	Hour	Summary of Events and Information	Remarks and references to Appendices
SUS ST LEGER	July 30th		Section to proceed to FROHEN LE GRAND. Soon after the A.D.V.S. visited the Section. Section moved at 12.50 p.m. The day was very hot and kept us trying to fit horses and men. Passed through IVERGNY, LE SOUICH and BOUQUEMAISON. When a halt was called and horses nosebags were inspected; everything was found to be in good order. After resuming the journey we passed through NEUVILLETTE. Before entering BARLY a steep winding descent had to be negotiated, then a rather rough surface of any awkward incident of any kind. At BARLY the Section halted for half an hour. Horses were watered then from MEZEROLLES an early was expected to RENAISNIL. AD. of 43rd b.f. Bde. for horses Section arrived at FROHEN LE GRAND at 5.45 pm and took up billets at 6.15 pm for excellent old leg been chosen. There was an abundant supply of water above at same from a running stream.	
FROHEN LE GRAND.	July 31st		A hut was erected for the men and several visits were paid. Lunch rations from AIX LE CHATEAU to complete for a range area in the morrow. Orders were received at midnight for section to proceed on the morrow to BERNAVILLE.	

J.W.W.W.M.

CONFIDENTIAL.
....

WAR DIARY.

of

26th Vet, Mobile Section.

August 1916.

(Volume   )

Army Form C. 2118.

WAR DIARY
or
INTELLIGENCE SUMMARY
(Erase heading not required.)

Place	Date	Hour	Summary of Events and Information	Remarks and references to Appendices
FROHEN LE GRAND	Aug. 1st		Reveille at 6 a.m. Left FROHEN LE GRAND at 9.15. a.m. following behind Div. H.Q's. Transport. A steep hill was encountered outside the village which was negotiated easily, although about 40 yards from the top I halted to give the horses their wind. The heat was very trying prepared baths were made. We passed through LE MEILLARD and arrived at BERNAVILLE at 11.45 a.m. The site chosen for me was not good being an orchard with the trees close together, water was near at hand. To-day I evacuated one horse to No 22. Vety Hospital (Mange).	
BERNAVILLE	2nd		Paraded men at 9 a.m. and issued Instructions to the N.C.O's + men re Sanitation in accordance with a memo received from Div. H.Q's. A.D.V.S visited the Section. Trucks were orders for horses at CANDAS. Col. L. Cunningham D.A.V.S. Reserve Army, visited the Section and inspected Section Horses which he said were looking "very well".	
"	3rd		Evacuated one horse and two mules to No 22. Vety Hospital from C.A.M.D.R.S. O.C. South Midland. Ml. V.S called + took from me two horses shod	

WAR DIARY
or
INTELLIGENCE SUMMARY

Army Form C. 2118.

Place	Date	Hour	Summary of Events and Information	Remarks and references to Appendices
	Aug 4th		Collected in BERNAVILLE. Inspected Gasmasks & goggles.	
	Aug 5th		Collected one mule by float from BOISBERQUES. Beaufresse Sent three horses to Candas for the Base, they stayed overnight there & waited for the following day's train, leaving at 3.p.m. ADVS notified Section. Received orders to move to COISY at 11.10 p.m.	
	6th		B/f Billets at 11.15 and marched whilst Div Train Passed thro' CANAPLES PLESSELLES. Sent in billeting party (Interpreter & one man) at 12.50 P.M. Arrived at Coisy at 7.30 p.m. Received orders 8.45 p.m. to march to ALBERT at 7.a.m.	
	7th		Reveille at 5.a.m. Left camp at 7.15 a.m. The day was cooler, the lorry traffic on the road created considerable dust, almost unbearable. Passing through QUERRIEU, joining main road at X roads North of PIERREMONT	

WAR DIARY or INTELLIGENCE SUMMARY

Army Form C. 2118.

Place	Date	Hour	Summary of Events and Information	Remarks and references to Appendices
ALBERT			BUIRE, DERNACOURT, and then over railway on side of a little about 2.R. S.W. of ALBERT. until 43rd Inf. Brig. Transport. Horse lines made with the wagons, lines under a wagon cover, fleeces water supply 1½ R. distant, impossible to obtain fine wild mounted horses fortunately no very lame horses were admitted so far. Made arrangements with Commd'ts for a leave of their water cart once daily.	
"	9th		Routine as usual. Inspected saddles & rifles. In evening went with my interpreter to find a more suitable place for the Camp; found one near the River at BUIRE Sur L'ANCRE, not far from rail head, which is MERICOURT A.D.V.S. visits section.	
			Reported location of suitable camp to A.D.V.S. Inspected goggles.	
"	10d		Raining. In the afternoon new lines were erected with posts lent to us by the Commdt R. Infantry. Sent to MERICOURT for wagons for the horses.	

WAR DIARY
INTELLIGENCE SUMMARY

Place	Date	Hour	Summary of Events and Information	Remarks and references to Appendices
ALBERT	Aug. 11		I travelled to home to the Base. Went to A.D.V.S. Office with weekly returns. During the evening the A.D.V.S. & myself, visited the place where the 17th Division M.V.S. was situated so as to have been ordered to take over from them. Found it very suitable, lines & standings. We shall be glad to hold Section horses, 2,233 ft for the men.	
	12		& very convenient to MERICOURT Station. Received instructions to establish an advance post on the morning. Day is very wet. A.D.V.S. visited the Station. Nine wounded horse received, some very lame, float cases.	
	13th		Reveille at 5.30 a.m. Sgt. Branded Pte Thompson, Pte Frazer were sent to take over the 29th M.V.S. advanced post I went with them, & was present at the handing over. The wounded horses were sent on to RIBEMONT (three float cases). Six were evacuated from MERICOURT. Full orderlies sent to advanced post, one to show the other the way, also to A.D.V.S. Office. One wounded horse brought down from advanced post.	

WAR DIARY or INTELLIGENCE SUMMARY

(Erase heading not required.)

Army Form C. 2118.

Place	Date	Hour	Summary of Events and Information	Remarks and references to Appendices
RIBEMONT	Aug 14		2nd M.V.S. have not moved yet, so am in a neighbouring wood. Showery day. Routine as usual.	
"	15th		Ordinary parade at 5 p.m. each evening for advance for hot ADVS's office. Saddle rifle inspection held. Two Routine as usual.	
"	16th		Evacuated 10 animals from MERICOURT to the Base. Visit by ADVS + Col Hunt (ADVS 4th Army).	
"	17th		Visited 14th Div Sys. advanced post, A.D.V.S	
"	18th		Went to HEILLY and drew 605 Francs for Pay of NCO's + men.	
"	19th		Ordered Boxes for horses to the Base. Routine as usual.	
"	20th		Evacuated 10 animals from MERICOURT. Visit by A.D.V.S. Sent ambulance to Ordnance Workshops HEILLY for repairs	
"	21st		2nd M.V.S. moves out, we take over their Pullets, the horse standings w/painted. Large hypsel? manure dip by other units, started on for removal as the flies are becoming a pest. Two bombs dropped within 25 yards	

Army Form C. 2118.

WAR DIARY
or
INTELLIGENCE SUMMARY
(Erase heading not required.)

Place	Date	Hour	Summary of Events and Information	Remarks and references to Appendices
Ribemont	2/2		Army advance post near BÉCORDEL, no damage done. Inspected saddlers rifles.	
"	23rd		Routine as usual. Visited 14 Div. Sig. Co. ADVS and advanced post. Visit by ADVS.	
"	24th		Tube helmet goggle inspection held. Ambulance returns repaired. Ordered wagons for sick horses. Evacuated 12 animals from MERICOURT.	
"	25th		Visit any Co. ADVS advanced post. Ordered wagons for same.	
"	26th		Evacuated 10 animals to the Base. Visit by ADVS.	
"	27th		Routine as usual. Have a fair number of sick horses as I have good accommodation for them, minor cases which would be well in a fortnight are kept, also those of course too ill to travel.	

WAR DIARY or INTELLIGENCE SUMMARY

(Erase heading not required.)

Army Form C. 2118.

Place	Date	Hour	Summary of Events and Information	Remarks and references to Appendices
RIBEMONT	28		Evacuated 7 animals to the Base. Visit by ADVS. Visited 14 Sig Co. tokaused Pat. Inspection of rifles, saddles.	
"	29		D.D.V.R. arrives to cast some horses. Routine as usual.	
"	30		Visit by ADVS. Routine as usual.	
"	31		Evacuated 13 animals from MERICOURT. Left Camp at 3.30 p.m. passed through AMIENS. arrived at ST SAVEUR. at 12.45. a.m. good billets for men & horses.	

F. J. Weir
Capt AVC
O.C.

WAR DIARY
or
INTELLIGENCE SUMMARY
(Erase heading not required.)

Army Form C. 2118.

Place	Date	Hour	Summary of Events and Information	Remarks and references to Appendices
ST SAVEUR	Sept 1st	9.30 a.m.	Left Camp at 9.30 a.m. for BOISRAULT passing through AILLY-SUR-SOMME POURDRINOY, OISSY, HORNOY. Arrived at 7.30 p.m. Very bad hill to climb. Found a barn for men — field for horses.	
BOISRAULT	2nd			
"	3rd		Saddle & rifle inspection. Tuck were charge of 43rd Brig. of Infantry. Went to a farm 3/4 mile from Boisrault found trouble, got permission from A.H.& N.9 Moved to FERME ST LARME, got accommodation for all. Good water supply, in Boisrault the water was very bad.	
FERME ST LARME	4th		Routine as usual. Went to BELLOY ST LEONARD — Div. H.Q. and AIRAINES as it was the nearest rail buy, only 20 K. from ABBEVILLE. Visit by A.D.V.S. Routine as usual. Visited the 43rd Brig.	
"	5th			
"	6th		Went to HORNOY drew 605 francs paid NCO's + men. Interpreter went to AIRAINES to arrange with the French railway authorities for the dispatch of sick horses as there was no R.T.O at that station.	
"	7th		Visit by A.D.V.S. Sent 6 animals to base via AIRAINES. Went through all the Vety. equipment drugs, instruments etc.	

WAR DIARY or INTELLIGENCE SUMMARY

Army Form C. 2118.

Place	Date	Hour	Summary of Events and Information	Remarks and references to Appendices
FERME ST. LARME	7th		Went to 43rd Brig. Routine as usual to remounts.	
"	8th		Routine as usual. Pointed the G.S. Limber + men booked it. MALLE INED to remounts.	
"	9th		The Helmet + gas goggle inspection. Painted R.S.P.C.A. ambulance. Received orders to proceed to AILLY SUR SOMME.	
"	10th		Struck camp at 10 a.m. Lep Ferme at 11.30 a.m., marched via L'ARBRES à MOUCHES, SOUES, PICQUIGNY. Arrived at AILLY at 9 p.m. Received orders to proceed to-morrow to BUIRE SUR ANCRE at 5.30 a.m.	
AILLY SUR SOMME	11th		Reveille at 4 a.m. Struck camp at 5 a.m. Marched at 5.30 a.m. via AMIENS, QUIERREU, LAHOUSSOYE. Arrived at QUIERREU at 11.30 a.m. bivouacced until 2.30 p.m. Watered & fed horses. Arrived at BUIRE at 5.30 p.m. Camped in the wood.	
BUIRE	12th		A.D.V.S + myself went to ALBERT to find a suitable site for the Mobile. decided on a camp ½ mile NE of DERNANCOURT. Huts were there for men + one tent, water amenable & section near the railway is a small hanre. This is somewhat an an here	

WAR DIARY or INTELLIGENCE SUMMARY

Army Form C. 2118.

Place	Date	Hour	Summary of Events and Information	Remarks and references to Appendices
BUIRE	12th		As we have no instruments, and watering available for showing, trimming & very lame horses. Before at hand	
			Left BUIRE at 9.30 p.m. arrived at ILLUS at 4 p.m. ADS & kitchens	
ALBERT	13th		ADVS this date arrived at Section testing as there is no room at FRICOURT CHATEAU. Conference attended by all the V.O's in the Division. Saddle & rifle inspection held.	
	14th		Got a quantity of ammunition boots shirts & hats. Went to FRICOURT to the H.Q. with ADVS, & sent to EDGE HILL to order wagons for the base.	
	15th		Sent 14 animals to the Base. I went to BÉCORDEL to put up an advanced post. Received 5 animals from the advanced Post. Shells fell in our area, one about 500 yds, no casualties. The R.S.P.C.A. ambulance shafts broken, this was caused by some horse cutting	

WAR DIARY or INTELLIGENCE SUMMARY

Army Form C. 2118.

Place	Date	Hour	Summary of Events and Information	Remarks and references to Appendices
ALBERT	15		staking up about 1½ m[iles] out of the ground, observing mines the position firing over the ANCRE, showing the horse in its head. The circle of this wagon is too low on the ground, the body being much slung, + is a good wagon for the Streets of London, but not for service, a few wheeled ambulance is in my opinion much more satisfactory in every way. Sent draft away at once to HEILLY to meet Supply Column. They will leave here ready to-morrow at noon.	
	16th		Sent for drafts to HEILLY. Received orders to proceed to FRICOURT with an advanced party. MAMETZ, but could not move just then, as the drafts had not turned up with my limber-wagons. The order however was cancelled + our Division was made to "Carry on" moving to its large number of casualties. Received orders however	

WAR DIARY
or
INTELLIGENCE SUMMARY

(Erase heading not required.)

Army Form C. 2118.

Place	Date	Hour	Summary of Events and Information	Remarks and references to Appendices
ALBERT	16.		to y Hd area in tr-mounts. Stella fell in we are in approx the afternoon, 2 § in ms. no casualties. Sunk to MERICOURT for wagons as way in were not available I EDGE HILL.	
	17th		Sent ambulance to FRICOURT for a horse. Went with the sick animals to MERICOURT. Picked up an ambulance case at EDGEHILL from a RESERVE PARK. The ADV.S took the remainder of the sick into their new billets at BUIRE. I returned to rest camp to look for the remainder of the equipment of the ambulance to reneurea to new billets. No sick horses received at the advanced post.	
BUIRE	18th		visit by ADVS. Saddle rifle inspection.	
	19th		Ordered trucks at MERICOURT. Sent one man to M.V.S. Guards. Divisin in accordance with instructions received from ADV.S. each section in sending a man these will act as an duty parties at the Base.	

WAR DIARY or INTELLIGENCE SUMMARY

(Erase heading not required.)

Place	Date	Hour	Summary of Events and Information	Remarks and references to Appendices
BUIRE	20th		Evacuated eighty animals to the Base withdrew to Advanced Post recently. to A.D.V.S. mule. Visit by A.D.V.S. Received instruction to proceed to TALMAS at 12.30.p.m. to morning. Withdrew my men from British Division M.V.S.	
"	21/12		Sent 1 S.D.B. MILL for three ullans for remounts. Six remounts arrive as the D.A.C. failed to turn up for them. Marched via LANOUSSOYE, BEAUCOURT VILLERS BOCAGE. The most muddy I have ever been in. The column was two hours late starting point. We took four hours to do six kilometres. The head of the column halted at BEAUCOURT for two hours to wait Head, it was 5.30.p.m. before we started again from LANOUSSOYE — OK. — from billets at BUIRE arrived at TALMAS at 11.30.p.m. Received orders to proceed to BREVILLERS to morrow. Starting at 8.a.m.	

WAR DIARY
or
INTELLIGENCE SUMMARY

Army Form C. 2118.

Place	Date	Hour	Summary of Events and Information	Remarks and references to Appendices
TALMAS	22		Left camp + struck in the road for D. known before the column started moving. Went via BEAUVAL (where we halted for 1½ hours mid-day feed) DOULLENS, GROUCHES, LUCHEUX, arriving at BREVILLERS at 6 p.m.	
BREVILLERS	23		Routine as usual. Took over charge of 2 + 3 Brig.	
—	24		Collected a horse at LUCHEUX. Went to the case at 10 D.L.I. at LE SOUICH. Saddle rifle inspection. Visit by ADVS. Took Helmer type goggle in action. Received orders to proceed to FOSSEUX via Sus ST LEGER, BARLY in the 27th inst. Went to Ivergny to an accident case at No 4 Co. A.S.C. Div.Train. Visit by ADVS.	
—	26		Went to Ivergny. Held P.M. on horse. Visit by ADVS.	

WAR DIARY
or
INTELLIGENCE SUMMARY
(Erase heading not required.)

Place	Date	Hour	Summary of Events and Information	Remarks and references to Appendices
BREVILLERS	27		Marched to POSSEUX leaving at 9.45 a.m. (IVERGNY). (Sus ST LEGER) (BARLY) Arrived at 1 p.m. with old vacated billets. Sector from the French. Stables have been built for Section & sick horses and a lot of improvements made. Sent to SAULTY for trumpeter.	
FOSSEUX	28		Sent 32 horses (other Dunning) to the Base from SAULTY. Went to AVESNES LE COMTE drew 840 francs for Pay of NCO's & men. Visit by A.D.V.S. Interprets gone on leave to Paris. Saddle trifle inspection. Routine as usual. Went to 43rd Bry also at BERNEVILLE.	
"	29			
"	30		Visit by A.D.V.S. Routine as usual.	

J. W. F.
Capt.
O.C.

WAR DIARY

of

26TH MOBILE VETERINARY SECTION.

October 1st 1916 to October 31st 1916.

Army Form C. 2118.

WAR DIARY
or
INTELLIGENCE SUMMARY
(Erase heading not required.)

Place	Date	Hour	Summary of Events and Information	Remarks and references to Appendices
FOSSEUX.	1/10/16	—	Sgt. BRUMHEAD admitted into hospital. Routine as usual.	1
"	2nd	—	Ordered wagon for Base at SAULTY. Visit by A.D.V.S. Repairs carried out in Lines & stables as it was raining very hard. Saddle rifle inspection.	
"	3rd	—	Visit to BERNEVILLE to 43rd Brig. Evacuated 8 animals to the Base from SAULTY.	
"	4th	—	Visit by A.D.V.S. appointed Town Major of FOSSEUX for a few days. Raining.	
"	5th	—	Ordered wagon for Base at SAULTY. Saddle rifle inspection. Visit to 61st Co RE & at SAULTY.	
"	6th	—	Evacuated twelve animals to the Base from SAULTY.	
"	7th	—	14 DAO arrive in town handed over Town Major to A.D.t. in D.A.C. Ordered wagon	

WAR DIARY or INTELLIGENCE SUMMARY

Army Form C. 2118.

Place	Date	Hour	Summary of Events and Information	Remarks and references to Appendices
FOSSEUX	7th		For sick horse at SAULTY. Interpreter M. DIDIER returns from leave.	
"	8th		Evacuated 40 animals to the Base. Visit by A.D.V.S. Capt CARROLL R.A.V.C. rides with me.	
"	9th		Ordered wagons for Base from SAULTY. Visit by A.D.V.S. Inspection of Gas Helmets & goggles. Saddle & rifle inspection.	
"	10th		Evacuated 64 animals to the Base from SAULTY.	
"	11th		Took over duties of A.D.v.S. Major DALGLIESH proceeds on leave to England.	
"	12th		Inspection of 7 & 8th Brig RFA at WANQUETIN with D.D.V.S. Cancelled. Went to TINCQUES distributed 2.3 remounts to the Division. Sent to SAULTY to order wagons for the Base.	

Army Form C. 2118.

WAR DIARY
or
INTELLIGENCE SUMMARY

(Erase heading not required.)

Place	Date	Hour	Summary of Events and Information	Remarks and references to Appendices
FOSSEUX	12th		Went to ADVS's Office at WARLUS. Evacuated 24 animals to the Base.	
"	13d		Sergt. Nolan AVC reports ferocity from No 7 Vety Hospital is pleasing. Sergt. Pomated examined unit of the area.	
"	14th		Returns examined out in stable floors, troughs. Went to 151 ARLUS. Chalk drawn from BERLY for stable floors + footpad.	
"	15		Went to WARLUS. Sent to North Hants Yeo. for 7 rem mts	
"	16d		Ordered wagons at Saulty. Saw R.S.P.C.A. two wheeled ambulance to the R.F.C. Have two fort whelspits in as it is too heavy for one horse. Saddle rifle topenein.	
"	17d		ADVS inspects 46th Bry R.F.A horses the DAC also the section. Evacuated 8 horses to the Base.	

WAR DIARY
or
INTELLIGENCE SUMMARY

Army Form C. 2118.

26th MOBILE VETERINARY SECT. No. 3 Date 1-11-16

Place	Date	Hour	Summary of Events and Information	Remarks and references to Appendices
FOSSEUX	18th		Inspection of DDVS for Div. Train enrolled. Inspected for ADVS the Corporation.	
"	19th		Ordered wagons for Base from SAULTY. Routine as usual.	
"	20th		Evacuated Horses to Base. No. S.E. WB. 4622 Pte CHILVER J.M. of the Section sent to No. 2. Vety. Hospital en route for England b/o a sergeant with a field unit. (ADVS memo No V 33 dated 18-10-16). Held P.M. on a horse: ADVS's inspection of Section Inv. + 44th Fd. Ambulance.	
"	21st		Wagon returns from 613 B R E with front wheels, looks very well + more arrivals. Routine as usual.	
"	22nd		Visit by ADVS. Went to WARLUS. Wagon ordered at SAULTY for Base. No 21822 Pte WEBB G.W. reports for duty from No 6 Vety Hospital. Saddlers rifle inspection.	

Army Form C. 2118.

WAR DIARY
or
INTELLIGENCE SUMMARY

(Erase heading not required.)

26th MOBIL
No. 2
Date 1-11-16
VETERINARY SEC[TION]

Place	Date	Hour	Summary of Events and Information	Remarks and references to Appendices
FOSSEUX	23rd	—	Visited by ADVS. Emanuel Eemonals to the Base. Cpl. Hobart a gyppie inspection. One Officers char 40 lb. sent to the Advanced Base Depot. (Memo No. 1575 dated 22-9-16 DDVS. 4th Army) in lieu of one small char. Satisfactory inspection.	
"	24	—	Cpl. Haynes of this Section proceeds to 41st Brig (2nd/1st) in Vety Sergt. has gone sick. Visited by ADVS.	
"	25	—	P.M. held on a horse which died of Genuponous pneumonia. Routine as usual. No 32114	
"	26	—	Visited by the ADVS. No 32114 Sergt. Roberts of this Section proceeds on special leave to England.	
"	27th	—	Visited by the ADVS. who gave me orders to proceed this morning to FILESCAMP. FARM. South With Party, who with Tracy place in respect, as I have to move to allow No 23 M.V.S. Section I arrived at	

WAR DIARY or INTELLIGENCE SUMMARY

Army Form C. 2118.

Place	Date	Hour	Summary of Events and Information	Remarks and references to Appendices
FOSSEUX	27		LATTRE ST QUENTIN. (A.K. from Villercarp Farm) where I mank your billets. Reported my position & ADVS by orderly.	
LATTRE ST QUENTIN	28th		Visit by ADVS. Took over charge of 8 & 3rd Brig.	
"	29		Went round units of 8 & 3rd Inf. Brig. BEAUFORT. AMBRINES. VILLERS SIRE SIMON. PENIN. DOFFINE FARM. IZEL LE HAMEAU.	
"	30		Saddle & rifle inspection Cpl Hoppin reporte from H.Q. 2nd Brig. Routine as usual.	
"	31		Ordered trucks at Savilly. Visited 43rd Brig. Billeted a mule to horse at BROUILLY. Fifty two francs from M. O'Strew for Kitchener Memorial Fund.	F.J.McEir RVC Capt

2449 Wt. W14957/M90 750,000 1/16 J.B.C. & A. Forms/C.2118/12.

Vol 18

Confidential
War Diary
of
Capt Weir A.V.C
O.C 26 Mob. Vety Section

From 1st Nov. 1916 to 30 Nov. 1916.

Volume no 4

Army Form C. 2118.

WAR DIARY
or
INTELLIGENCE SUMMARY

(Erase heading not required.)

Instructions regarding War Diaries and Intelligence Summaries are contained in F. S. Regs., Part II. and the Staff Manual respectively. Title Pages will be prepared in manuscript.

[Stamp: 26th MOBILE VETERINARY SECTION No. 1 Date 31-11-16]

Place	Date	Hour	Summary of Events and Information	Remarks and references to Appendices
LATTRE ST. QUENTIN.	1/11/16		A.D.V.S. visited. 8 sick animals evacuated to the Base from SAULTY.	
"	2nd		Visited 43rd Brig. Routine as usual.	
"	3rd		Went to H.Q. at Le CAUROY. Routine as usual.	
"	4th		One mule executed at ETRÉE WAMIN.	
"	5th		Saddle & rifle inspection. Wagon overhaul at SAULTY for sick horses.	
"	6th		Sent 16 animals to the Base from SAULTY. S/E No. 7008 LLOYD Pte. G.H. meets with an accident, whilst driving the horse ambulance to SAULTY.	
"	7th		Went to BEAUFORT & GIVENCHY LE NOBLE 43rd Brig. Inf. Picured rain all day. Received orders to proceed to FARM. MONT JOIE 5K. north of Frévent.	
"	8th		Started with Section to FARM MONT JOIE at 11·30 a.m. Arrived at 5·30 p.m.	

WAR DIARY
or
INTELLIGENCE SUMMARY
(Erase heading not required.)

Army Form C. 2118.

Place	Date	Hour	Summary of Events and Information	Remarks and references to Appendices
LOOOUSE FARM MOUNT JOIE	8th		Rained all day. Everybody wet through. Very indifferent billets for men & horses. Left three horses with 2.3. M.V.S. before leaving for new billet.	
"	9th		Went to BUNEVILLE + PETIT HOUVIN. 4 - 3rd Sq. Brig. Wagons washed, billets & stables fair in order. Tube helmet inspection.	
"	10th		Went to SIBEVILLE + HOUVIN - HOUVIGNEUIL. Saw a horse at a farm left behind by the 20th Middlesex ordered in to the Short. Col. HARVEY. D.D.R. 3rd ARMY. visits Section. SE No 3216. Sergt. Roberts. R. returns from leave from England.	
"	11th		Sent 1 H.Q. Horse and 3 Riders to Remount Section 3rd Army. Ordered one wagon at FREVENT for the Rear. S.E. No 4135. Pte HARVEY. T. AVC reports for duty from NO.2. V. Hospital.	
"	12th		8 animals evacuated from FREVENT. Visit by ADVS. S.E. NO 4555 Pte ADAMS. W. sent to NO.2. Vety. Hospital (DDVS 3rd ARMY Memo No V/133 dated 8/11/16. he being too old to stand the work of the Section during the winter months.	

Army Form C. 2118.

WAR DIARY
INTELLIGENCE SUMMARY

Place	Date	Hour	Summary of Events and Information	Remarks and references to Appendices
FARM MOUNT JOIE	13d		Evacuated 6 animals to the Base from PREVENT. Saddle & rifle inspection. Visit by the ADVS.	
"	14d		7 animals collected at REBREUVIETTE. 4 animals at PETIT BOURET SUR CANCHE. 2 animals at ETREE WAMIN. 2 animals at GRAND BOURET SUR CANCHE. Ordered 3 wagons at PREVENT.	
"	15d		1 animal an ambulance was collected at GRAND BOURET SUR CANCHE. 3 animals at CONCHY SUR CANCHE collected. 72 animals collected at VACQUERIE LE BOUCQ. 3 animals at CONCHY SUR CANCHE. Evacuated 22 animals to the Base from PREVENT. Only ways to to 5 mmm.	
"	16d		Evacuated 15 animals to the Base. Five animals collected at AUBROMETZ. Sent ambulance to AUBROMETZ to bring in back.	
"	17d		Visit by ADVS. Routine as usual. Ordered one wagon at PREVENT.	
"	18d		Evacuated seven animals to the Base.	

Army Form C. 2118.

WAR DIARY
or
INTELLIGENCE SUMMARY

(Erase heading not required.)

Instructions regarding War Diaries and Intelligence Summaries are contained in F. S. Regs., Part II. and the Staff Manual respectively. Title Pages will be prepared in manuscript.

[Stamp: 26th MOBILE VETERINARY SECTION No. 4 Date 31-11-16]

Place	Date	Hour	Summary of Events and Information	Remarks and references to Appendices
FARM MOUNT JOIE	19/11/16		Evacuated two mangy cases to the Base. Visit by ADVS & AAHQMG. S.E. NO. 2008. Pte SWAYNE. M. leaves Section for DDVS's office 1st ARMY wd V/A/OH. (Authority AVC Base Records T/5/780/16.)	
— " —	20/11/16		Went to Burnville held a P.M. on one H.D. horse belongs to No 1. C. Div. Train. attached to 11th K's Regt, found rupture of double colon. Went to 8 & 9 Co R.E. in MONTENERVOIS. Went to 43rd Field Ambulance at Petit Houvin. No. 1012 Pte JOHNSON. J.R. rpt wts for duty from No 6 V.H. One horse collected at HAUTE VISÉE.	
— " —	21st		Sent for wagon to FREVENT. Visit by ADVS. One animal evacuated at ROZIERE. Evacuated 8 animals to the Base from FREVENT. Soldale rifle inspection.	
— " —	22nd		Visited 11th K's R. Regt. at BUNEVILLE. Went to Div. H. Qrt. Le CAUROY.	
— " —	23rd		Paid NCO's & men. 280 Francs. Gas helmet inspection held.	

WAR DIARY or INTELLIGENCE SUMMARY

Army Form C. 2118.

Place	Date	Hour	Summary of Events and Information	Remarks and references to Appendices
FARM MOUNT JOIE	24th		Two animals collected at ROUBERS SUR CANCHE. Sent horse away to PREVENT for the Base.	
"	25th		Visit by ADVS. Three horses collected at REBREUVE SUR CANCHE. Evacuated 8 animals to the Base from PREVENT. Four men sent to 43rd Field Ambulance to be inoculated with T.A.B. vaccine.	
"	26th		Two animals collected at REBREUVE SUR CANCHE. One horse at MUNCR collected.	
"	27th		Evacuated 8 animals to the Base from PREVENT. Two animals collected at REBREUVIETTE collected. One animal at LIGNY SUR CANCHE. 1 animal at REBREUVE SUR CANCHE. 4 men sent for inoculation with T.A.B. SE NO 8357. Pte WILLIAMS F. reports for duty from No 13 V.H.	
"	28th		Two animals collected at CONCHY SUR CANCHE.	
"	29th		4 men sent for inoculation to 43rd F.A. Evacuated 1 animal with Strangles from PREVENT. SE. NO 3657. Pte COOMBES EA. proceeds on leave to England.	
"	30th		One horse collected at GOUY EN TERNOIS. One horse collected at 28 Souich Nord 4 DVS.	

O.C. 26 m.v.S.

Vol 19

<u>Confidential</u>

War Diary
of
<u>O.C. 26th Mobile Veterinary Section</u>

From 1st December 1916 to 31st December 1916

(Volume No. 12)

Army Form C. 2118.

WAR DIARY
or
INTELLIGENCE SUMMARY

(Erase heading not required.)

26th MOBILE VETERINARY SECTION No. 1 Date 3/1/17

Instructions regarding War Diaries and Intelligence Summaries are contained in F. S. Regs., Part II. and the Staff Manual respectively. Title Pages will be prepared in manuscript.

Place	Date	Hour	Summary of Events and Information	Remarks and references to Appendices
FARM MONT-LA-JOIE	1/12/16	—	Visited 43rd Infantry Brigades at Bienville & Moncheaux Huruin Houvepril and also the 89 Coy RE at Sercourt. Sent to Trevent to collect wagons for the Base	
"	2nd	—	Evacuated 8 Animals to No 22 V.H. from Trevent. Sent one Rider to the Remount Depôt 3 Army. Renew floor of stable with Bue No. One h/60 and three men inoculated with T.A.B.	
"	3rd	—	Collected one horse from Louvetille 1.2 miles NE of Lt. Col. Park and rifle on shelter	
"	4th	—	Routine as usual No 12/2/16 Ste Barnes W. proceeded on leave & the United Kingdom. Visited by the A.D.V.S. Sent to Trevent to obtain Wagons for the Base	
"	5th	—	Evacuated 9 Animals to the No 22 V.H. from Trevent. Went to the "H" Dec 54 R. Vet with A.D.M.S. Orders Boxes for the Base One h/20 and three men inoculated with T.A.B.	
"	6th	—	Evacuated 8 Animals to the No 29 V.H. from Trevent of Col Sgt. C Blanc W. proceeded on leave to the United Kingdom	
"	7th	—	Collected one horse from Boulers and 3/cm Corch Sun-banch Visited by the A.D.V.S.	
"	8th	—	Enlisted 3 horses from Entrée — Women Routine as usual	
"	9th	—	Visited 43rd Inf Brigades Visited by the A.D.V.S. Base Requisition and Tube Helmet and etc Pass people conductor Evacuated 19 Animals to the No 22 V.H. from Trevent. Drew 10.00 Francs from the Cashier Paid: £20.00 MEN	1

2449. Wt. W14957/Mg0 750,000 1/16 J.B.C. & A. Forms/C.2118/12.

WAR DIARY
or
INTELLIGENCE SUMMARY
(Erase heading not required.)

Army Form C. 2118.

Place	Date	Hour	Summary of Events and Information	Remarks and references to Appendices
FARM Mont la Joie	10/12/16	—	Collected 3 horses from Entrée-Wamin which were ambulance cases. Stable and Rifle inspection. Evacuated 8 animals to No 22 V.H. from FREVENT. Collected 2 horses left in view-carré and one at Blangerval also went to Boubers sur Canche. One broke but these animals have been collected by the 3 Mob.V.Section.	
"	11"	—	Men & O Coup. Collated me a stable at Frevent. Evacuated 7 animals to No 22 V.H. from Frevent	
"	12"	—	Visited by Left. Thornwill A.V.C. Routine as usual. Evacuated 7 animals to No 22 V.H.	
"	13"	—	Visited by the A.D.V.S. Routine as usual	
"	14	—		
"	15	—	Visited 11" Trips. depot and the 43" Div. amt Ambulance. Evacuated 7 animals to No 22 V.H. from Frevent. Destroyed one L.D. horse to 50" Bty R.F.A. 9" Div. Suffg from the evgos	
"	16"	—	Visited by the D.D.V.S. and A.D.V.S. Stables and Rifle inspection.	
"	17"	—	Evacuated one animal to No 22 V.H. from Frevent. Received to 40 Billets at Favieul on the 19".	
"	18"	—	Evacuated 3 animals to No 22 V.H. from Frevent. Collected one animal from Fortel.	
"	19"	—	Struck camp at 7A.M. Left Mont la Joie storm at 9.30A.M. proceeded to Favieul via Pollincourt and Burg arrived Favieul at 1.4 P.M. Collected one horse from the village of Rebreuve. Capt. T. Thornwill A.V.C. and two servants came to reside with Section.	

WAR DIARY or INTELLIGENCE SUMMARY

Army Form C. 2118.

Place	Date	Hour	Summary of Events and Information	Remarks and references to Appendices
FOSSEUX	20/12/16	—	Routine as usual. Reference to the Stable Roof and Floor and decay up of Butter which was in a bad state	
"	21"	—	Visited by the A.D.V.S. Refixing of Stable etc Saddle and Rifle inspection SE/1/1789 Pte Amos W.F. Refuses to two Mmts for Duty from s/31. V.H. s/SB 19526 FRANKLIN of the Sent proceeded to s/31 K.H. for Duty. SK/6063657 Boomles T.A. 99m sent to Hospital Sick. Sent to duty to 1st Doc Bosses for the Base	
"	22"	—	Evacuated 8 Animals to s/1822 V.H. from Saulty. Visits by the A.D.V.S. Drew 900 francs from the Field Cashier Late of Pro Ruhin.	
"	23"	—	Routine as usual. Refixing of Stable continues. Doe Reparator and S20 Administration	
"	24"	—	Visited by the A.D.V.S. Routine as usual	
"	25"	—	Routine as usual. Sent to Saulty to 1st Doe Bosses for the Base	
"	26"	—	Evacuated 13 Animals to s/1822 V.H. from Saulty. SK/6063651 Pte Boomles Evacuated out of the area.	
"	27"	—	Visited by the A.D.V.S. Sent to the G.R.E. Park Saulty for canvas etc for the Stables	

Army Form C. 2118.

WAR DIARY
or
INTELLIGENCE SUMMARY

(*Erase heading not required.*)

Place	Date	Hour	Summary of Events and Information	Remarks and references to Appendices
FOSSEUX	28/10/16		Routine as usual	
"	29"		Refixing of Stable Flooring Etc. Visited by the ADVS	
"	30"		Visited by the ADVS. Routine as usual	
"	31"		Visited by the ADVS. Saddle and Rifle inspection in loopt. Weir proceeded on leave to the United Kingdom. loopt. Leavoroll takes over the Leton Durry. loopt. Muir a Lonce	

[signature]

Vol 20

Confidential

War Diary
of
O.C. 26th M.T.S.

From 1st Jany 1917 to 31st Jany 1917

(Volume No 44)

Army Form C. 2118.

WAR DIARY
INTELLIGENCE SUMMARY
(Erase heading not required.)

Place	Date	Hour	Summary of Events and Information	Remarks and references to Appendices
FOSSEUX	1/1/17		Visit by ADVS. Sent to SAULTY to order wagons for the Base.	
"	2/1/17		Visit by ADVS. Evacuated 17 animals to the Base. SE 2711 Pte KEMP reports for duty from No 9. V.H.	
"	3/1/17		Routine as usual. Visit by ADVS	
"	4th		Sent to Saulty for wagons. Road made down to the Stables.	
"	5th		Visit by ADVS. Evacuated 12 animals to the Base.	
"	6th		Stalls not received. Floor repaired. One horse destroyed A/52 R77 opening from held.	
"	7th d.		Stones carted for stables. Visit by ADVS. Saddle rifle inspection.	
"	8th		Visit by ADVS. One of our own draught horses died on f.m. a large calculus was found in large ulcer.	
"	9th		Sent to Saulty to draw wagons for the base. Ditto gun a/b harness is special. Evac. 11 animals to the Base.	
"	10 d.		Visit by ADVS. Received orders to move at Hellis by noon to-morrow	

WAR DIARY or INTELLIGENCE SUMMARY

Place	Date	Hour	Summary of Events and Information	Remarks and references to Appendices
FOSSEUX	11th		Routine as usual. Capt WEIR returns from leave. Sent to Saulty to order wagon from the Base	
"	12th		Same. 11 animals to the Base. Visit by ADVS.	
"	13th		Routine as usual.	
"	14th		Visit by ADVS. Sent to Saulty to order wagons for the Base. Small rifle inspection held.	
"	15th		Same. 12 animals to the Base.	
"	16th		Left personal billet went to live in a hut built by the Coys. made arrangements through the ADVS & DDVS. that we were to stay at FOSSEUX. Went to H.Q. to a court of Inquiry to investigate the loss of a mule from this Section when at "En vrai Joie Ferme." Drew 850 francs for pay of NCO's + men.	
"	17th		Sent to Saulty for wagon. Routine as usual	

WAR DIARY
INTELLIGENCE SUMMARY

Army Form C. 2118.

Place	Date	Hour	Summary of Events and Information
FOSSEUX	18th		Evacuated one animal to the Base. Visit by ADVS. Went to Remount depot at FREVENT.
"	19th		Evacuated 3 animals to the Base. Routine as usual
"	20th		Took over Vety charge of 4th Corps.
"	21st		Visit by ADVS. Clipped 3 horses at B&H.Y. with mange belonging to the Enfiereine than Saddle & rifle inspection held.
"	22nd		M. DIDIER Interp. returns leaves section to report for duty at French Mission. Horses at Barly washed & dressed with Calcium Sulphide.
"	23rd		Visit by ADVS. Section horses manes & tails trimmed. Routine as usual.
"	24th		Routine as usual. Anti-gas appliances inspected.
"	25th		Routine as usual. Water wagons at Saulty.
"	26th		Evac. one animal to the Base. Visit by ADVS.

WAR DIARY or INTELLIGENCE SUMMARY

Army Form C. 2118.

Place	Date	Hour	Summary of Events and Information	Remarks and references to Appendices
FSSevel	27th		Routine as usual. Received orders to send no more horses to the Base for a few days.	
"	28th		Visit by ADVS. Destroyed one animal belonging to 105 M.R.C. in P.M. Also two Sikh guns mares septic & badly wounded.	
"	29th		Destroyed one mule belonging "G" Battery R.H.A. P.M. Septic corono-pedal joint. Saddle & rifle inspection held. Sauter-inch Mange.	
"	30th		Sirce. 2 animals to the Base from Sauter-inch Mange. Visit by ADVS. Destroyed one animal belonging to 9 C.R.E. with Tetanus but Picked up mail: Septic arthritis, having not all mud enough.	
"	31st		Routine as usual. ADVS proceeds to Esquimalt on leave. Taken over from him.	

Y.J.W.E___
Captain
O.C.

Vol 2<u>nd</u>

<u>Confidential</u>

War Diary

of.

<u>O.C. 26th M.V.S.</u>

"From 1st February '17 to 28th February '17.

(Volume No. ~~#6~~)

Army Form C. 2118.

WAR DIARY
or
INTELLIGENCE SUMMARY
(Erase heading not required.)

Place	Date	Hour	Summary of Events and Information	Remarks and references to Appendices
FOSSEUX	1/2/17		Went to Div. H.Q. Went to see a sick cow at DAINVILLE as report of French mission.	
"	2/2/17		Went to Div. H.Q. Routine as usual. Visit 7th Corps.	
"	3/2/17		Civilian mange horses dressed with Col. Stephoke at BARLY. Routine as usual. Railway closed for transport of sick horses until further orders.	
"	4/2/17		Saddle & rifle inspection. Went to 1st Cav. Div. Reserve Park at Barly under orders from D.V.S. 3rd ARMY to hold an inspection.	
"	5/2/17		Went to Div. H.Q. Routine as usual. Visit 7th Corps.	
"	6/2/17		Repairs in stalls floor carried out. Wagons washed. Routine as usual.	
"	7/2/17		P.M. held on a horse with Smith. Railway opened. Ordered three wagons from SAULTY. Visit 7th Corps.	
"	8/2/17		Evacuated totally amicle & chulier horse killer to the Base. Went to Div. H.Q. Went to D.A.D.O.S. Office. Routine as usual.	

Army Form C. 2118.

WAR DIARY
or
INTELLIGENCE SUMMARY
(Erase heading not required.)

Place	Date	Hour	Summary of Events and Information	Remarks and references to Appendices
POS SEWOC	9th		One horse collected at SARS LES BOIS. Travelling very difficult owing to heavy conditions of the roads. Routine as usual.	
"	10th		Saddlery/a materiel held also gas apparatus in operation. W/Out to D.V.H.Q.	
"	11th		Insp. in charge of 278 Co. R.E. WANQUETIN. A.D.V.S. returns from leave. Inspec. 7th Corps H.Q. horses.	
"	12th		Went to 27, S.G.R.E. WANQUETIN. Remount co. wane. Water Carriers fitted on waggons.	
"	13th		Visit by A.D.V.S. Supt. Corps A.V.C. proceeds to No 2. V.H. for duty. Take over charge of 41, 2nd Inf. Brig. SOMBRIN + GRAND ROULLECOURT. Visit 7th Corps.	
"	14th		Sent to SAULTY for waggons. Visit 41 & 2nd Inf. Brig.	
"	15th		Evacuated 25 animals + 3 hides to the Base.	
"	16th		Horse dance to a Pack operation. Visit by A.D.V.S. Visit 7th Corps. The baggage waggon team to the train is definitely to draw [?] 20/Oct [?]	

WAR DIARY
or
INTELLIGENCE SUMMARY

Army Form C. 2118.

Place	Date	Hour	Summary of Events and Information	Remarks and references to Appendices
FOSSEUX	16th		Wood for the Division. Supplies line not to be drawn in horse ambulance.	
-//-	17th		Went to 10 August to 278 Co R.E. Routine as usual.	
-//-	18th		Sergt Roberts + 2 privates proceed to ABBEVILLE as escort for A/Cpl ASHWORTH. + Pte THOMPSON. who are held in custody at that place. Visit 41st Inf. Brig.	
-//-	19th		Visit 7th Corps. Routine as usual.	
-//-	20th		Visit by ADVS. Saddle + rifle inspection.	
-//-	21st		Ordered 3 wagons from SAULTY. Routine as usual.	
-//-	22nd		Evacuated 21 animals to the Base + killed. I am detailed as prosecutor on a G.C. one at BARLY for trial of a Cpl. Yc of German Prisoner. Visit 7th Corps.	
-//-	23rd		Visit by ADVS. Visit 41st Inf BRIG. Routine as usual.	
-//-	24th		Anti Gas appliance inspection. Went to Ambulette 278 Co. R.E.	
-//-	25th		Routine as usual. Visit 7th Corps.	

Army Form C. 2118.

WAR DIARY
or
INTELLIGENCE SUMMARY
(Erase heading not required.)

Instructions regarding War Diaries and Intelligence Summaries are contained in F.S. Regs, Part II. and the Staff Manual respectively. Title Pages will be prepared in manuscript.

Place	Date	Hour	Summary of Events and Information	Remarks and references to Appendices
PISSEUX	26th		Visit by ADMS. Baggage wagon returns from Train, an ambulance wagon is not satisfactory.	
"	27th		Wear AUBIGNY. Arrange for entraining of sick horse. Visit 7th Corps. Take over charge of C.C.S. 3rd from Rains Batt. at Grand Rullecourt.	
"	28th		Visit by ADMS. Evacuated 17 animals to the Base viâ 2 hides from AUBIGNY. Visit H.Q. Brig.	

F.J. West
Capt AVC
O.C.

Confidential

War Diary
of
O.C. 26th M.V.S.

Volume 46
(Mar: 1st to Mar 31st 1917)

WAR DIARY
or
INTELLIGENCE SUMMARY.

(Erase heading not required.)

Place	Date	Hour	Summary of Events and Information	Remarks and references to Appendices
FossEux	1/3/17		Evacuated two horses from Sanity to the Base. Operated on an Orgoena case, trephined skull. Visit by ADVS.	
"	2/3/17		Routine programme changed to	
			Reveillé – 6. a.m.	
			Exercise 6.30 — 7.30 a.m.	
			Stables Wat'r feed 7-35 a.m.	
			Tie away 7-40.	
			Breakfast 7-45	
			Parade 9. a.m.	
			Grooming, Sick horses 9 — 11.30 a.m.	
			Saddlery 11-30 — 12 mid-day	
			Wat'r feed 12-45 p.m.	
			Dinner 1 p.m.	
			Fatigues 2-30 — 4 p.m.	
			Wat'r feed 4.30.p.m.	
			Tea 5.30.p.m.	
			Hay up. (9. p.m.)	

Army Form C. 2118.

WAR DIARY
or
INTELLIGENCE SUMMARY.
(Erase heading not required.)

Instructions regarding War Diaries and Intelligence Summaries are contained in F. S. Regs., Part II. and the Staff Manual respectively. Title pages will be prepared in manuscript.

[Stamp: 26th * VETERINARY SECTION * No. 2 Date 31-3-17]

Place	Date	Hour	Summary of Events and Information	Remarks and references to Appendices
OSSEUX	3/3/17		Visit 7. Corps H.Q. Visit 41st Inf. Brig.	
"	4/3/17		Capt. Dunlop-Martin A.V.O. Took over charge of VII Corps H.Q. Visit 278. Road Construction Co. R.E. Routine as usual.	
"	5 do		Saddle tupé inspection. Visit by A.D.V.S.	
"	6 do		Visit 41st Inf. Brig. All wagons worked. Routine as usual.	
"	7 do		Ordered wagons from Sawills. No. SE 10502. Cpl. Lavurne of the tanks at own request. Visit by A.D.V.S.	
"	8 do		Evacuated 10 animals to the Base + sick lines.	
"	9 do		Destroyed one animal for debility. No.w. 278 C.R.E. Gas helmet + appliances inspection held, two were found unserviceable.	
"	10 do		Visit 41st Inf. Brig. Visit by A.D.V.S. Brake fitted in the R.S.P.C.A ambulance.	1st Wart
"	11 do		P.M. held on a horse died with colic. Routine as usual.	

A5834 Wt. W4973/M687 750,000 8/16 D. D. & L. Ltd. Forms/C.2113/13.

Army Form C. 2118.

WAR DIARY
or
INTELLIGENCE SUMMARY.
(Erase heading not required.)

Instructions regarding War Diaries and Intelligence Summaries are contained in F. S. Regs., Part II. and the Staff Manual respectively. Title pages will be prepared in manuscript.

Place	Date	Hour	Summary of Events and Information	Remarks and references to Appendices
FOSSEUX	12/3/17		Sent for horse ambulance. Visit by A.D.V.S. Saddle & rifle inspection held.	
"	13d		Visit 278 Co R.E.	
"	14d		Visit by A.D.V.S. Routine as usual.	
"	15d		Visit by A.D.V.S. Visited 41st Inf Brig at BERNEVILLE.	
"	16"		Went to Basly to examine some of the inhabitants horses for attaque. Drew money for pay of 2/2.C.O. & Men. Sent to auth 12 or O.C. Horses for the Bask destroyers are stoice suffering from Tetanus. Visito by the A.D.V.S. Evacuates 33 & animals to the Base from Southgrave 6 Hdes	
"	17"		SE1799. Pte AMOS. W. F. promoted Corporal	
"	18"		Visits of the A.D.V.S. Routine as usual Fatigues washing wagons etc.	
"	19"		Routine as usual Visits to the A.D.V.S.	
"	20"		Took over charge of the VII Corps Sent to Chromode fonte to arrange with the O.C. of II. M.V.S. to Evacuate to 3 Mange basis from Tangers	

J.W.E.

Army Form C. 2118.

WAR DIARY
or
INTELLIGENCE SUMMARY.
(Erase heading not required.)

Place	Date	Hour	Summary of Events and Information	Remarks and references to Appendices
FOSSEUX	21"		Evacuated 3 animals to the Base from Tangues. Visits to the 41st Inf. Bgd.	
"	22"		Visits the VII Corps. Visit by the A.D.V.S.	
"	23"		Visits 278 by R.E. Sacola & Rifle inspection	
"	24"		Visit by the A.D.V.S. Sent to South to over look cases for the Base. Visits the VI Corps. State Gas appliances inspection all in good condition. Evacuates 61 animals to the Base from South. Sent 9 horse shoes.	
"	25"		Visits by the A.D.V.S. Took over charge of the 43rd Inf. Brig. Visits 278 by R.E. Visits the VI Corps. Attended to Maj. Tavenham horse which was very ill with colic. Visits the 43rd Inf. Brig. Attended one horse with colic	F.J.S.(?) Captain
"	26"		Routine as usual. Visit by the A.D.V.S.	
"	27"		Sent to Ostrebury to ortu cases for the Base	

WAR DIARY
or
INTELLIGENCE SUMMARY.

(Erase heading not required.)

Army Form C. 2118.

Place	Date	Hour	Summary of Events and Information	Remarks and references to Appendices
FOSSEUX	28/3/17		Evacuated 45. Animals to the Base from Saulty. Drew one dog. Iron Rations for the section from Simencourt. Sent 15 Horse Hides to 022 Veterinary Hospital	
"	29"		Routine as usual. Visited by the A.D.V.S.	
"	30"		Sent 1 daily 1000 Roses for the Base. Received orders for move to Simencourt.	
"	31st		Evacuated 69 Animals to the Base from Saulty. Visited by the A.D.V.S. Went over to Simencourt to take over new Billet.	

Signed
Capt a.v.c.

Vol 23

Confidential

War Diary

of

O.C. 26th M.V.S.

April 1st to April 30th '17

(Volume 47)

Confidential

Army Form C. 2118.

WAR DIARY
or
INTELLIGENCE SUMMARY.
(Erase heading not required.)

Instructions regarding War Diaries and Intelligence Summaries are contained in F. S. Regs., Part II. and the Staff Manual respectively. Title pages will be prepared in manuscript.

Place	Date	Hour	Summary of Events and Information	Remarks and references to Appendices
FOSSEUX	1st		Sent 1 N.C.O. + 2 men to new billet, as I was unable to move the Section, my men being at the Base with horses. Twenty two horses wanting the French arrange for the 40 Infantry to dig a hole for them.	
—	2nd		As the horses are not wanted I leave the Sectional them in the hands of the Camp Commandant 7th Corps. We move out to new billet at Simencourt 11.30 a.m. very cold + stables empty arrived at Simencourt at 1. p.m. good stables + good billets for men; the place is a sea of mud + water is not close at hand for sick lines as carriage for the Boom is a walk cart from 4 to 8 B.A.C.	
SIMENCOURT	3rd		Stables refound, + the place cleaned up. Visit by A.D.V.S. Received orders to pick out an advanced post at DAINVILLE.	
—	4th		Went to DAINVILLE with Sergt. Roberts, fixed on a site suitable for advanced post. Visit by A.D.V.S. Road Rec'd promo from evacuation of sick horses on Monday, Wednesday + Saturday each week. Favoured 40 animals to the Base. P.M. held on four debility cases which destroyed the S. Tetanus. Ham was found in the mesenteric artery + in the lumen wall, + the S. Arnati him in large numbers.	
—	5th		In jacket mudif proof coats returned to Ordnance. Visit by A.D.V.S. Routine as usual. Drew 800 francs for pay & N.C.O.'s + men.	

Army Form C. 2118.

WAR DIARY
or
INTELLIGENCE SUMMARY.
(Erase heading not required.)

Place	Date	Hour	Summary of Events and Information	Remarks and references to Appendices
SIMENCOURT	6th		Arranged with C.R.E. to supply 6 picketing posts for the advanced posts. These will be drawn from the Park at DAINVILLE. Collected waggons at YOUY for sick horses.	
"	7th		Sent advanced post to DAINVILLE. Saw them fixed up there. Evacuated 67 Animals with Base and 37 Ridges.	
"	8th		Routine as usual. Visit by ADVS. Ordered Trucks at YOUY. Collected from advanced post in the evening.	
"	9th		Evacuated 50 animals to the Base and sick. Routine as usual. 1 NCO + 10 men report for duty from No.1 V.H. to act as Conducting party to the Base, as my own men are unable to cope with the demands.	
"	10th		No appliances available. Routine as usual. Ordered waggons at YOUY for sick horses. Collected from advanced post.	
"	11th		Evacuated from YOUY 38 animals + 12 hides. Routine as usual. Visit by ADVS. Collected from advanced post.	
"	12th		Went to advanced post. Routine as usual.	
"	13th		Received orders to proceed to STONY D'ENCOURT. Went there + found the place full of troops no billets available. Was directed by 4.3rd Bde H.Q. to proceed to LE CAUROY, found good billets + stables. Sent on an advance party to take them over. Troops in advanced post this evening.	
"	14th		Evacuated 40 animals to the Base from YOUY + 9 hides. Conducting party transferred to 1/1 Northumbrian Division. M. V. D.	

WAR DIARY
or
INTELLIGENCE SUMMARY.
(Erase heading not required.)

Army Form C. 2118.

Place	Date	Hour	Summary of Events and Information	Remarks and references to Appendices
SIMENCOURT.	15th		Marched to LE CAUROY at 1. p.m. Raining very hard, went via WANQUETIN AVESNES LE COMTE. arrived at 4. p.m.	
LE CAUROY	16th		Unloaded wagons, saddlery + harness cleaned + inspected, all sick line had collars washed + greased. Sent an ambulance to BARLY. Sent 14 birds to RTO BOUY. Visit by ADVS.	
"	17th		Wagons washed + overhauled + greased. Sent to FREVENT for wagon for sick horses Staff over change of 42. 2nd Brig. 612nd Co + 62nd Co. RE + 2nd Field Ambulance, +2 2nd M.G. Co. + 3rd Cav. Div. Am. Sub Cy. Went to collect horses at BOUBERS	
"	18th		Evacuated 51 animals to the Base. Conchy Sur CANCHE, FREVENT, LIGNY SUR CANCHE VACQUERIE LE BOUCQ. six horses in all, nine horses were dead. Visit by ADVS.	
"	19th		Visit the unit under my charge. Routine as usual.	
"	20th		One horse evacuated at MONT.EN.TERNOIS. Routine as usual. Sent to FREVENT for wagons.	
"	21st		Evacuated 12 animals to the Base. Visit by ADVS. Visit units in my charge. SE N° 6/65 Pte WILSON.W reported to the ADVS as being absent, not having returned with the undertaking party from the Base.	MWSh A/Capt
"	22nd		Wagon returned at FREVENT. Visit #3rd Brig. Received orders to proceed to FOSSEUX.	
"	23rd		Evacuated 8 animals to the Base + collected one animal at REBREUVE. Marched at	

A5834 Wt. W4973/M687 7,30,000 8/16 D. D. & L. Ltd. Form/C.2118/13

WAR DIARY
or
INTELLIGENCE SUMMARY.

(Erase heading not required.)

Army Form C. 2118.

Place	Date	Hour	Summary of Events and Information	Remarks and references to Appendices
LE CAUROY	23rd	1 p.m.	for FOSSEUX. arrived at 4 p.m. managed to get the old stables and billets. Gas appliance inspection.	
FOSSEUX.	24th		Received orders at 4.30 a.m. to proceed to BELLACOURT, starting point wind mill FOSSEUX-GOUY road at 6.30 a.m. marched out at 6.25 a.m. arrived at BELLACOURT at 1 p.m. No stables horses picketted in the open, men in bivouac. Rugs dumped at FOSSEUX. Weather good.	
BELLACOURT	25th		One horse collected at BASSEUX. by lorries. Visit by ADVS. Saddle & rifle inspection. Wagons washed. Received orders to proceed to BERNEVILLE on the 26th. 900 francs drawn for pay of NCO's & men.	
"	26th		Marched to BERNEVILLE both men billetted from 1/1 Northumbrian M.V.S. 35 horses were handed over to me, and 1 N.C.O. & 10 men conducting party.	
BERNEVILLE	27th		Sent to GOUY to order wagons. Stables cleaned out & repaired. Routine as usual.	
"	28th		Evacuated 32 animals + 2 no. hides to the Base. Routine as usual.	
"	29th		Went to ACHICOURT. found a position for advance post. Sent out advance Post at 5.30 p.m. Sent ambulance to TILLOY for a wounded horse. Visit by ADVS. Sent to GOUY for wagons.	

WAR DIARY
or
INTELLIGENCE SUMMARY.

(Erase heading not required.)

Army Form C. 2118.

Place	Date	Hour	Summary of Events and Information	Remarks and references to Appendices
BERNEVILLE	30		Went to SIMENCOURT to get permission to use road which is closed to Govt. for walking cases, as it is a long distance for debility horses through Beaumetz. Sent to Advanced Post. 18 horses evacuated to the Base from Gouy.	

F.J.W.E.
Capt AVC
O.C.

Vol 24

Confidential

War Diary
of
O.C. 26th M.V.S.

From May 1st to May 31st 1917.

(Volume 48)

Confidential

War Diary
of
O.C. 26th M.V.S.

WAR DIARY
or
INTELLIGENCE SUMMARY.
(Erase heading not required.)

Army Form C. 2118/3/17

Instructions regarding War Diaries and Intelligence Summaries are contained in F. S. Regs., Part II. and the Staff Manual respectively. Title pages will be prepared in manuscript.

Place	Date	Hour	Summary of Events and Information	Remarks and references to Appendices
BERNEVILLE	1/5/17		Sent to Gouy to order wagons for the Base. Repairs in sick line floor carried out. Sent to advance post at 5 p.m.	
"	2/5/17		Evacuated 59 animals to the Base from Gouy. Routine as usual. Sent to Advance Post at 5 p.m.	
"	3rd		Ambulance repaired. Visit by ADVS. Routine as usual. Sent to Advance post 5 p.m.	
"	4th		Sent 3 privates to the 7th Corps M.V.S. under instructions from ADVS. Routine as usual. Ordered wagons at Gouy. Sent to Advance Post 5 p.m.	
"	5th		Visit by DDVS. Evacuated 16 animals and one line to the Base.	
"	6th		Pte Kemp evacuated sick Sent to Advance Post 5.p.m. Saddle & rifle inspection. Ordered wagons at Gouy. Sent to Advance post 5.b.m.	
"	7th		Sent to Advance post at 10.a.m. Evacuated 13 animals.	
"	8th		Ordered wagons at Gouy. Instr new duties of ADVS. Major DALGLEISH sent to no 1 comp at BARLY.	
"	9th		Evacuated 10 animals to the Base from Gouy. Went to see ADVS at BARLY.	
"	10th		Drew 700. Francs for pay of NCO's + men at FOSSEUX. Went to Div. H.Q. ARRAS. Anti-gas appliances inspected. SE No. 4 & 7 Pte SAUNDERS.G reports for duty from No. 2. Vety. Hospital. Horse respirators rendered unserviceable to be returned to S.H.R. Depot ABBEVILLE.	Capt

WAR DIARY
or
INTELLIGENCE SUMMARY.
(Erase heading not required.)

Army Form C. 2118.

Place	Date	Hour	Summary of Events and Information	Remarks and references to Appendices
BERNEVILLE	11th		Sent to GOUY to order wagons. Saddle & rifle inspection. Sent to Advanced Post.	
"	12th		Visit by Acting D.D.V.S. Major CONDER, made inspection of sick & section lines, received instructions as I was acting D.D.V.S. to move the Mobile to a forward position & evacuate from ARRAS. Went to Div. H.Q. arranged with A.A.+Q.M.G. about the proposed move, received orders to proceed to AGNY on the 15th inst. 13 animals evacuated to the Base from GOUY. S.E. NO. 72.11 Pte KEMP. J. evacuated out of the area suffering from septic hand. Sent to Advanced Post 5 p.m.	
"	13th		Went to see ADVS at BARLY. Ordered wagons for the Base. Sent to Advanced Post.	
"	14th		Evacuated 27 animals to the Base from GOUY. Visit H.Q. at ARRAS. Sent to Adv. Post. Went to AGNY to find billets for section. I take over billets vacated by 18th Div. Gr. N.S., leaving behind one NCO + 3 men mounted	
"	15th		Section moves to AGNY, to clean up lines, billets. Marched out at 9.30 a.m. arriving in new billets at 12.30 p.m., the billets is good, water in the billets for horses, brick standing for foot cases, good billets for NCO's + men. The A.D.V.S's clerk taking mouse in to same billet, the H.Q. are leaving ARRAS to-day. Sergt dating back to April 9th. Sergt NOLAN promoted S/Sergt	

A.S.834. Wt. W4973/M637. 750,000 8/16 D.D. & L. Ltd. Forms/C.2113/13.

Army Form C. 2118.

WAR DIARY
or
INTELLIGENCE SUMMARY.

(Erase heading not required.)

Instructions regarding War Diaries and Intelligence Summaries are contained in F. S. Regs., Part II. and the Staff Manual respectively. Title pages will be prepared in manuscript.

Place	Date	Hour	Summary of Events and Information	Remarks and references to Appendices
AGNY.	16th		Drew the Advanced Post from ACHICOURT. Billets cleaned up, lines erected. Billets in a very dirty condition Manure deposited in several places etc.	
"	17th		Routine as usual cleaning up camp. Visited the ADVS at BARLY. Great difficulty recuperating wagons	
"	18th		Sent to ARRAS for wagons. Saddle triple inspection.	
"	19th		Evacuated 20 animals to the Base from ARRAS.	
"	20th		Routine as usual	
"	21st		Received orders for the attached men (1 NCO + 10 men) to return to the Base. ADVS returns from hospital + resumes duty.	
"	22nd		8 men. belonging to remounting party return to the Base, the other 3 are at the Base with horses. Sent to ARRAS to order wagons.	
"	23rd		Evacuated 7 animals to the Base. 3 privates, remainder of remounting party attached return to No 1 V.H. Corpl. Amos W.E. proceeds to England on special leave	
"	24th		Wagons overhauled + painted. Ambulance sent to supply column to supply column to be overhauled.	

Army Form C. 2118.

WAR DIARY
or
INTELLIGENCE SUMMARY.
(Erase heading not required.)

Instructions regarding War Diaries and Intelligence Summaries are contained in F.S. Regs., Part II. and the Staff Manual respectively. Title pages will be prepared in manuscript.

Place	Date	Hour	Summary of Events and Information	Remarks and references to Appendices
ARMY	25th		Sent to ARRAS to draw bones for the Base. Saddle & rifle inspection.	
-"-	26th		At 10.30.p.m. German aeroplane bombed the camp around, & bombs fell in an empty space about two hundred yards from Sikkim billet. Evacuated 28 animals to the Base and two kids from ARRAS. Operated one animal with a growth wound. Take over charge of 11th King's Liverpool Regt.	
-"-	27th		Drew 750 Francs for pay of N.C.O's & men. Sergt Nolan's appointment cancelled at his own request. S.E. No: 487 Pte SANDERS. G. admitted to hospital.	
-"-	28th		Routine as usual S.E No 7371 Pte JONES I.R. reports for duty from No.1.V.H.	
-"-	29th		Routine as usual.	
-"-	30th		Inspected horses of 11th King's Liv. Regt.	
-"-	31st		Routine as usual. Spotted mare here forth weeks - a remount -	

WAR DIARY or INTELLIGENCE SUMMARY

Army Form C. 2118.

Place	Date	Hour	Summary of Events and Information	Remarks and references to Appendices
A.G.N.Y.	1/st		Routine as usual. Sent to ARRAS for horses for the Base. Visit by A.D.V.S.	
-"-	2nd		R.S.P.C.A. ambulance repaired by 11th Kings Liv. Regt. Evacuated 15 animals to the Base from ARRAS. Aeroplane raid at 10.15 p.m. 4 bombs fell in dyke 300 yards from billet, no damage done.	
-"-	3rd		Saddle & rifle inspection. Routine as usual. Air raid again at 10.35 p.m. no damage done.	
-"-	4d		S.E. No. 10502. Pte. LAWRIE. J. proceeds on leave to U. Kingdom. 10 men from 14 Div. Employment Co. report to this unit to remove stacks of timber & manure left in billet. 43 & Field Ambulance take a large quantity of material from billet + remove it. Air raid took place at 10.15 m.g. no damage done.	
-"-	5-		Sent to ARRAS to order horses for the Base. Air raid takes place again at midnight. Pen's fire in transport lines with machine gun. Receive orders to evacuate establishment by 5 riders.	
-"-	6d		Evacuated 11 horses to the base from ARRAS. Station shelled o/s. horses were housed no damage done.	

A.D.V.S.

WAR DIARY or INTELLIGENCE SUMMARY

Army Form C. 2118.

Place	Date	Hour	Summary of Events and Information	Remarks and references to Appendices
AYN	7th		Routine as usual. Fatigue party finish the cleaning up of billet. Started painting the transport. Garage with B. Echelon 14 D.A.C.	
"	8th		to lend me a wagon to draw supplies during the painting. Sent to ARRAS to order boots for the Base.	
"	9th		Two saddles trades returned to Ordnance stores. Evacuated one animal to the Base from ARRAS. Gas appliance inspection. BM	
"	10th		ADVS Cavs Section the Div. H.Q. moved to-day for rest area. Received orders to proceed to MONCHIET on the 13th inst. Saddle & rifle inspection. Drew 1650 francs for pay of NCO's & men. Ordered boots at ARRAS for the Base	
"	11th		Evacuated 10 animals to the Base + 2 kicks 1 case Glanders reported by ADVS 56th Div. Received orders from ADVS to inspect all animals of 142nd Bry. which were drinking out of the same trough for any clinical case. No S.E. 16086 Pte. PARTINGTON. W. returns to duty from No 4 VET. Hospital.	

FMcE

Army Form C. 2118.

WAR DIARY
or
INTELLIGENCE SUMMARY.
(Erase heading not required.)

Instructions regarding War Diaries and Intelligence Summaries are contained in F. S. Regs., Part II. and the Staff Manual respectively. Title pages will be prepared in manuscript.

Remarks and references to Appendices

Place	Date	Hour	Summary of Events and Information
AGNY.	12th		Examined all animals of 43rd Brig. of Infantry & loaded. One German aeroplane brought down near ARRAS station whilst chucking the fire of a heavy gun, which shelled the station & HAICOURT every morning at 8 a.m. whilst the train etc. re-filling.
"	13th		Reveille at 4.45 a.m. Marched out at 9 a.m., arrived at MONCHIET at 12.30 a.m. Received orders to move to LARBRET in the 14th instant over to animals to H North ward in M.V.S. who are just opposite leave in reserve.
MONCHIET	14th		Marched out at 8 a.m. 10.10 a.m. arrived at LARBRET. Received orders to march to ST LEGER LES AUTHIE on the 15th. Billeting party consisting of one corporal + man proceed to Bus to meet the billeting officer.
LARBRET	15th		Left LARBRET at 8 a.m. arrived at ST LEGER LES AUTHIE at mid-day, billeting last day.
ST LEGER & LES AUTHIE	16		Visited by ADVS. No. 8E 4558. PTE W.R. MITCHELL proceeds on leave to U. Kingdom.
"	17th		Saddle rifle inspection. Inspected 43 d Inf. Brig. with ADVS. at carried MALLE IN VEST.

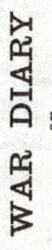

Army Form C. 2118.

WAR DIARY
or
INTELLIGENCE SUMMARY.
(Erase heading not required.)

Instructions regarding War Diaries and Intelligence Summaries are contained in F.S. Regs., Part II. and the Staff Manual respectively. Title pages will be prepared in manuscript.

Place	Date	Hour	Summary of Events and Information	Remarks and references to Appendices
ST. LEGER LES AUTHIE	18th		Finished Mallein testing 43rd Inf. BRIG. with the ADVS. Suggested we move nearer railhead as SAULTY is 15 K. and CANDAS very 20 K.	
"	19th		Visited 11th Kings Div. 43rd Inf. BRIG. and H.Q.	
"	20th		Routine as usual. Mallein tested 43 M & Co. with ADVS.	
"	21st		Routine as usual. Visit 43rd Inf. BRIG.	
"	22nd		Routine as usual. Visit 43rd Inf. BRIG. + 11th Kings Div.	
"	23rd		Routine as usual	
"	24th		No 1012. PTE JOHNSON. J. proceeds on leave to U. Kingdom. Sent to SAULTY broken lorch for the Base. Saddle troop inspection. Anti-gas appliance Inspection. Re-painted the R.S.P.C.A. for the Div. Show. Destroyed one animal of 11th Kings Div. p.m. held b/enlist one animal for Sunderbeck. Drew 800 francs for pay of NCO'S + men.	

Army Form C. 2118.

WAR DIARY
or
INTELLIGENCE SUMMARY.
(Erase heading not required.)

Instructions regarding War Diaries and Intelligence Summaries are contained in F.S. Regs., Part II. and the Staff Manual respectively. Title pages will be prepared in manuscript.

Place	Date	Hour	Summary of Events and Information	Remarks and references to Appendices
ST LEGER les	25		Evacuated 10 animals to the Base from SAULTY. Visit by ADVS.	
AUTHIE	26.		14 Div Show. Entered the ambulance, but was beaten for 3rd prize by an ambulance of 4.3st Field Ambulance	
"	27		Sent an ambulance to A.E.M for a horse. Visit by ADVS. visit 43rd Brig	
"	28		I take over duties of ADVS. 11th Kings Liv. Regt + 43 m. V.C.	
"	29.		Visit a.w.H.Q. Sent to Saulty for wagons for stores. wagons waited.	
"	30		Evacuated 8 animals to the Base from Saulty. Visit to l.O. w. Train + 43rd Field Ambulance	

J. Justin
Captain
OC. 26 m. V.S.

[Stamp: 26th MOBILE VETERINARY SECTION No. 3/6/ Date]

Vol 26

<u>Confidential</u>

War Diary
of
<u>O.C. 26th M.V.S.</u>

July 1st to July 31st 1917

<u>(Volume 50)</u>

WAR DIARY or INTELLIGENCE SUMMARY.

Place	Date	Hour	Summary of Events and Information	Remarks and references to Appendices
ST. LEGER LES AUTHIE	1/7/17		S.E. No 6740. Cpl. HAYNES. H.R. proceeds on leave to England. Saddle & rifle inspection. Went to Div. H.Q.	
"	2nd		Went to Div. H.Q. Routine as usual. Visit 43rd Brig. + C. Train.	
"	3rd		Routine as usual.	
"	4th		Visit H.Q. Routine as usual.	
"	5th		Visit to C. Div. Train. 43rd Brig. Routine as usual.	
"	6th		Sent to SAULTY 6 order boxes for the Base. Went to Div. H.Q. No. 601. P/A/Sgt. NOLAN. W. promoted to S/Sergt.	
"	7th		Visited 43rd M.G.Co. Evacuated 17 animals to the Base from SAULTY. This station is no longer available.	
"	8th		Saddle & rifle inspection. Visit Div. H.Q. Visit to C. Train and 43rd Brig. Received warning orders for move.	26/7/17
"	9th		Anti-gas appliances inspection S.E. No 30447 PTE. ISGATE. C. proceeds on leave to England. Collected one mule left at ST AMAND. Received orders to move to YEZAN COURT near DOULLENS on the 10th inst.	

WAR DIARY
or
INTELLIGENCE SUMMARY.
(Erase heading not required.)

Army Form C. 2118.

26th Mobile Veterinary Section (stamp)

Place	Date	Hour	Summary of Events and Information	Remarks and references to Appendices
ST. LEGER LES AUTHIE	10th July		Marched out at 9.30.a.m. via AUTHIE - THIEVRES - AUTHIELE arrived Gezaincourt at 3.30.p.m.	
GEZAINCOURT	11th		Drew 510 francs @ DOULLENS to pay NCOs & men. Left at 6.p.m. arrived CANDAS for entrainment @ 8.p.m. started loading Train left at 10.51.p.m. arrived BALLIEUL at 5.30.a.m.	
ST JANS CAPPEL	12th		Arrived at Billets 9.a.m. no billets were allotted to me, picked a nice billet which had been occupied by 48th M.V.S. near Corps Horse dip. Town shelled. Visit by D.D.V.S. Air raid at 9.p.m. and again at 3.a.m.	
"	13th		Routine as usual. Visited 2nd Inf. Brig. Visited by H.D.V.S. and D.D.V.S. Received orders to send 4 men to 9th Corps Veterinary detachment. Air raid at 3.a.m.	
"	14th		Proceeded on leave to Ireland from 15th to 25th Capt. J. O'Connell takes over Section during my absence.	

P.W.E.

WAR DIARY
or
INTELLIGENCE SUMMARY.

(Erase heading not required.)

Army Form C. 2118.

Place	Date	Hour	Summary of Events and Information	Remarks and references to Appendices
ST. JANS CAPPEL	15th		Saddle & rifle inspection. 4 men sent to Corps detachment.	
"	16th		No. 673 P/A/Sergt. CARD. R. AVC reports for duty from No 4. V.H.	
"	17th		Routine as usual.	
"	18th		SE No 4512. PTE RAIN E.R.W. proceeds on leave to Scotland. Returned all anti-gas goggles. Visited by Q A D V S.	
"	19th		Visit by Q ADVS routine as usual.	
"	20th		Routine as usual	
"	21		— : — : —	
"	22		Saddle & rifle inspection. ST JANS. CAPPEL bombed at 3.30 a.m.	
"	23		Visit by ADVS & ADVS.	
"	24		Anti-gas appliance inspection. SE No 4593 PTE JACKSON G.A. proceeds on leave.	
"	25		Visit by ADVS & ADVS. 1 mule destroyed & skinned, fractured ulna.	

Army Form C. 2118.

WAR DIARY
or
INTELLIGENCE SUMMARY.

(Erase heading not required.)

Instructions regarding War Diaries and Intelligence Summaries are contained in F.S. Regs., Part II. and the Staff Manual respectively. Title pages will be prepared in manuscript.

Place	Date	Hour	Summary of Events and Information	Remarks and references to Appendices
ST JANS CAPPELL	26th		Sent 4 horses supplies complete to 9th Corps School of Instruction for the day. Routine as usual.	
"	27th		Visited by Gen. Skinner. Capt W.En returns from leave. Visited by A.D.V.S.	
"	28th		Visited HQ 2nd Inf Brig. Routine as usual.	
"	29th		Routine as usual. Visit by D.D.V.S.	
"	30th		Routine as usual. Visit by D.D.V.S. & A.D.V.S. Drew 745 francs for pay of N.C.O & men	
"	31st		S.E. No 4135 Pte HARVEY. T. proceeds on leave. Visit by D.D.V.S. & A.D.V.S. Evacuated 21 animals to Base by road. (Ken mange cases)	

F. J. E. Capt.

Vol 27

<u>Confidential</u>

<u>War Diary</u>
<u>of</u>
<u>O.C. 26th M.V.S.</u>

From Aug 1st to Aug. 31st 1917.

(Volume No 51)

WAR DIARY
or
INTELLIGENCE SUMMARY.

(Erase heading not required.)

Army Form C. 2118.

6th MOBILE VETERINARY SECTION

Place	Date	Hour	Summary of Events and Information	Remarks and references to Appendices
ST. JANS CAPPEL	1/8/17	-	Routine as usual. Visit by DADVS.	
-"-	2nd	-	Visit by ADVS + DADVS. Routine as usual.	
-"-	3rd	-	Visit by DADVS. Routine as usual. Weather very bad.	
-"-	4th	-	Visit by DADVS + DDR. 15 p.c.o out Remounts (Surplus Riding of the Division)	
-"-	5th	-	Evacuated 14 animals to 9th Corps M.V. Detachment. Visit by DADVS. Sent 10 animals to No 2 Field Remount Section La BREARDE. Four men return from the Corps mobile Detachment. It will be noted that from July 15th, 15 August 5th when my four men returned from the Corps M. Detachment, they evacuated 14 animals for this Section. Received orders to move to PRADELLES on the 6th inst.	
-"-	6th	-	Reveille at 4.30 a.m. marched out at 9 a.m. Via Bailleul. Arrived at new fields at 1 p.m.	
PRADELLES	7th	-	Rifle + saddle inspection. Routine as usual.	
-"-	8th	-	Wagons washed etc. Visit by DADVS. Visit Sharps at La BREARDE and 9/2 K.R.R. at LE PEUPIER. Adss 4/14 Div Farm.	

4/8/17

WAR DIARY
or
INTELLIGENCE SUMMARY.

(Erase heading not required.)

Army Form C. 2118.

Place	Date	Hour	Summary of Events and Information	Remarks and references to Appendices
PRADELLES	9th		Visit Div. Train, 4 & 2 Inf. BRIG. Bombed by the Huns at 2 a.m. HAZEBROUCK shelled. Evacuated 1 mange case by road.	
"	10th		Visit by D.A.D.V.S. Visit Ox & Bucks. 42 M.Y.Co. found five horses were wounded the night before, the bomb fell about 20 yards from the lines. Gas appliances in operation. No 9 F 4655 Pte ASHWORTH T proceeds on 10 days leave to Scotland. Visit 41 Inf. Brig. 3/14 Train, 43rd Field Ambulance. 42 m y Co. 9 RB sent 6 mules, mines to remounts.	
"	11th			
"	12th		Visit by A.D.V.S. Operated on a mule. Routine as usual	
"	13th		Went to Div. H.Q. Drew 520 francs for pay of NCO's & men. Visit Train. 42nd & 44th Field Ambulances. Sent ambulance to collect a horse at BERTHEN.	
"	14th		Visit 3/Train 19th KRR at BORRÉ + 42nd M Y Co. Cpl. Harper proceeds on lillebring party destination unknown. Evacuated by fine animals by Road	AWR Capt.
"	15th		Reveillé S.a.m. Marched out 9 a.m. via Felbe, JODVAERVELDE + ABBELE. Arrived in billet at 1.30 h.n. taking over from 18th Div. m V.S. Visit by D.A.D.V.S.	

WAR DIARY
or
INTELLIGENCE SUMMARY.

(Erase heading not required.)

Army Form C. 2118.E

Place	Date	Hour	Summary of Events and Information	Remarks and references to Appendices
Sheet 27 L24 c.2.9.	16th		Saddle trifle inspection. Routine as usual.	
"	17th		Visit by ADVS. Went to RENINGHELST. with DADVS to see 56 Div. M.V.S. from which I propose to take over when they leave. Received mules & men to 2nd Corps M.V. Detachment, & put out an advance Post at DICKEBUSCH 1 NCO + 3 men; Sent Ambulance to fetch one animal from PRADELLES. Went to DICKEBUSCH to chose a place for Ad. Post. Found a suitable site near water about 50 yards from the Church. Pte. THOMPSON. J.A. proceeded on leave to Manchester.	
"	18th		One animal destroyed, stunned & twitch. Sent 1 NCO + 2 men to Ad. Pst. as three could not be spared.	
"	19th		Sent 2 more men to 2nd Corps M.V.D. as they are overcrowded with horses. Bombed at 9.30 p.m.	
"	20th		Routine as usual. Visit by DADVS. Ambulances going all day to the Div Train were bombed. 78 casualties. Operating all day removing pieces	

Army Form C. 2118.

WAR DIARY
or
INTELLIGENCE SUMMARY.
(Erase heading not required.)

Place	Date	Hour	Summary of Events and Information	Remarks and references to Appendices
Sheet 27 L24C.2.9.	21st		Ambulances going all day. Evacuated 12 animals to 2 Corps. M.V.Q. Visit by DADVS. One horse shot & one destroyed.	
"	22		Sent for 4 ambulance cars to 56 Div. M.V.S. as their ambulance had broken down. Evacuated 14 animals to the Base by Road. Established & relieved by Stitchers. Visit by DADVS Spratt on several animals. P.E. BARNES returns from Att. Prtn. as we were working at high pressure, also 2 men from C.M.D. which I had sent. Collected one ambulance case from Att. Post also one from 1 Aust. Div.	
"	23		Visit by DADVS + ADVS who informs me to evacuate all animals to the Corps. M.D.J. visit Corps. M.D. find there 250 horses + 15 men. Capt Bowen is unable to take my horses. Evacuated 24 animals to the Base by Road. + collected 2 ambulance cases.	
"	24		Gas offensive in Sector. Collected 2 ambulance cases. Operated on several animals with shrapnel wounds. 2nd Corps. M.V.D.	

Army Form C. 2118.

WAR DIARY
or
INTELLIGENCE SUMMARY.
(Erase heading not required.)

Place	Date	Hour	Summary of Events and Information	Remarks and references to Appendices
Steenw. 2.9.	24		Closed down, a case of Lampas being found at ST. OMER. Received a Soyer stove & 2 horse troughs, which we must make/take at the above, as we require a lot more for dressing purposes.	
-"-	25		Evacuated 12 animals to the Base by Road. Collected 4 ambulance cases. Visit by DADVS.	
-"-	26		Visit by DADVS. Advance Post withdrawn. Destroyed one animal.	
-"-	27		SE 3566 Pte Impey proceeds on leave to the U.K. Evacuated 13 animals to the Base by rail. Supplied in spection. Sent 38 hides to rail head. Supplied 9 men for Class A + B	
-"-	28		Evacuated 20 animals to 2nd Corps. M.V.D. Visit by DADVS. Warning order to move received. Sent 2 animals to Field Remount Station. Received orders to move to FLETRE.	
-"-	29a		Marched out at 10 a.m for FLETRE arrived at 2 p.m. Medical inspection of men.	
-"-	30		Visit by DADVS. Routine as usual.	
-"-	31		Routine as usual.	

Vol 28

"Confidential

War Diary

of

O.C. 26th M.V.S.

September 1st to 30th 1917.

(Volume No. 52)

WAR DIARY
or
INTELLIGENCE SUMMARY.

(Erase heading not required.)

Army Form C. 2118.

Place	Date	Hour	Summary of Events and Information	Remarks and references to Appendices
FLETRE	1/9/17		Exercised 10 animals 15th Bray by Road.	
"	2nd		Saddle rifle inspection. Went to Div. H.Q. Drew 900 francs from Cashier BAILLEUL for pay NCO's + men. Received orders to move to Sheet 28. S 29 a.2.b. Taking over from 2 Australian D.V. M.V.S. Air raids all night, his bombs dropped 150 yds from billets no damage.	
"	3rd		Routine as usual. Paid NCO's + men. Sent in NCO + 1 man billeting party.	
"	4th		Struck camp moved off at 10 a.m. via BOULOGNE BAILLEUL. Arrived at billet @ 2.15. p.m. Evacuated 1 horse to base by motor ambulance, horse ran back when almost in + fell on his back in the road, some side grease is required. On arrival at billets found the Australians had left + shorty before, it is a splendid place but requires a lot of hard work.	
Sheet 28. S29a.24.	5th		Visit by A.D.V.S. 8th Corps. Orders 14 Div. Srd'de training plans for of Shaths	

Army Form C. 2118.

WAR DIARY
or
INTELLIGENCE SUMMARY.
(Erase heading not required.)

Instructions regarding War Diaries and Intelligence Summaries are contained in F. S. Regs., Part II. and the Staff Manual respectively. Title pages will be prepared in manuscript.

Place	Date	Hour	Summary of Events and Information	Remarks and references to Appendices
Sheet 28 S.29.a.2.4.	6th		Wagons washed. Repairs in flow of stable. SE No 4808. PTE THOMPSON, F.A. admitted into Hospital sick.	
"	7th		Visit by DADVS. Repairs carried on.	
"	8th		Sent to R.E. Park to draw 500 sand bags + tarpaulin to make a drag + harness, also the huts in accordance with G.R.O's. Drew autumn coal draught in.	
"	9th		Visit by DADVS. Entrance bridge repaired, repairs in flow carried up.	
"	10th		Visit by DADVS. Visit to 2nd Ind. Brig SE No. 3704 S/S MITCHELL A. Gas appliance in sperita. Saddlet proceeds on leave to U.K. title no section.	
"	11th		Examined 2 + 3 animals to the Base by road. Visit by DADVS. Repairs carried out.	
"	12th		Operated on some animals. Repairs carried out. Sent ambulance to METEREN for a horse.	
"	13th		Sent SE.NO. 3566. PTE IMPEY. J. for examination Class B. Visit by DADVS. Repairs carried out. SE No. 4808. Pte M Thompson F.A. evacuated out of the area.	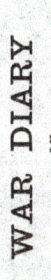

ns regarding War Diaries and Intelligence

WAR DIARY
or
INTELLIGENCE SUMMARY.
(Erase heading not required.)

Army Form C. 2118.

Place	Date	Hour	Summary of Events and Information	Remarks and references to Appendices
Sheet 28 S 29.a.2.4.	14th		Evacuated 5 animals to the Base by barge from 3 AC SAINT MAUR. also evacuated 12 animals to the Base by road. Received notice to obtain Barge, wire orders 8th D in on Sunday for Tuesdays sailing & Wednesday for Fridays sailing.	
"	15th		P.m on a heavy draught which died on the resent of a bomb wound received about an hour before at DICKIE BUSCH, found pus in chest Repairs in camp carried on.	
"	16th		No. 689 PTE BUSHBY. W.D. proceeds on leave to U.K. 17th—27th inst. Evacuated 16 animals to the Base by road. Saddle rifle inspection. Drew 800 francs for pay of NCO's men. Sent to 89 C.R.G. beyond NEUVE EGLISE for bricks for floor of stalles Visit by D.A.D.V.S. Paid NCO's & men.	
"	17th			
"	18th		By order of the A.D.V.S. all Bran & linseed to be visied from here, a good improvement. Evacuated 10 animals to the Base by Barge. Repairs carried on.	
"	19th		Lieut 846. Dr. THOMAS. A.S.C. proceeds on leave to U.K. from 20th—30th inst. Sent for horse to 9th Corps Horse D Pd. for whitewashing stables Repairs carried on. Received orders to send two men to Boulogne N.E. is long trek remounts for 2 chestp. Gunn.	

Army Form C. 2118.

WAR DIARY
or
INTELLIGENCE SUMMARY.
(Erase heading not required.)

Place	Date	Hour	Summary of Events and Information	Remarks and references to Appendices
Sheet 28 S29.a.2.4	20th		Two men entrain at BAILLEUL for BOULOGNE. Rest for evacuation of sick animals by road will be No5. Advance Sick Horse Holt. Rouge Croix. (Sheet 27 W10.c.11.) on Friday only the following day No 2. Sick Horse Holt. new EBBLINGHEM (Sheet 27. T.30 a.6.9.). 3rd Day ST. OMER. No 23.V.H. Sent for more tricks for repairs, tarring & whitewashing of stables continued.	
"	21st		Evacuated 2 animals by road (Mange). Visit 44th Field Ambulance.	
"	22nd		Repairs to billet carried on. Routine as usual.	
"	23rd		Saddle & rifle inspection. Col BARTLETT. AVC	
"	24th		Anti. gas appliance inspection. Commenced carting manure from large heaps left new stables. Repairs carried on. Visit 44th Field Ambulance.	
"	25th		Drew more bricks, repairs carried on. Visit DAVIS. at H.Q. who is ill.	
"	26th		Repairs carried on, still eating manure. Routine as usual.	
"	27th		Visit 44th Field Ambulance. Stoba we change of Div Train Capt O'CARROLL proceeds on leave to IRELAND.	

Army Form C. 2118.

WAR DIARY
or
INTELLIGENCE SUMMARY.
(Erase heading not required.)

Instructions regarding War Diaries and Intelligence Summaries are contained in F. S. Regs., Part II. and the Staff Manual respectively. Title pages will be prepared in manuscript.

Place	Date	Hour	Summary of Events and Information	Remarks and references to Appendices
Shed. 28 & 29 A.2.4.	28th		Evacuated 16 animals to the Base by Barge, also 5 hides, and three many ears to the Bevely road. Visit D.W. Train.	
— " —	29th		S.E. No 34-33. PTE COX. E. reports for duty from No 2. U. V. Repairs carried on.	
— " —	30th		Sent to 89 Co R.E. for canvas, stan for a stable. A big air raid took place, 5 bombs fell about 500 yards away, no damage caused, whether all fell in an open field.	

[Stamp: 26th MOBILE VETERINARY SECTION No. 5]

AWE
Captain
OC

[Stamp: 26th MOBILE VETERINARY SECTION No. 5 Date 1/10/?]

Vol 29

Confidential

War Diary

of

O.C. 26th M.V.S.

From Oct 1st to Oct 31st 1917

(Volume No. 53)

WAR DIARY or INTELLIGENCE SUMMARY.

Army Form C. 2118.

Place	Date	Hour	Summary of Events and Information	Remarks and references to Appendices
Sheet 28 S 29.a.2.4.	1/10/17		Routine as usual. Ground the NCOs & men a half day for Div. Trans. Sports, four Section horses entered for the jumpings.	
—"—	2nd		Visited Div. H.Q. Routine as usual.	
—"—	3d		Repair Standings carried out, bricks drawn from new BAILLEUL.	
—"—	4d		Visit to Div. Train. Repairs carried out, stables whitewashed & tarred.	
—"—	5d		No. SE 2809. Pte. SMARTT, R.R. proceeds on leave to U.K. 6th – 16th Oct. Visited by D. A.D.V.S. Evacuated 6 animals to Vet. Base, by Barge and one Mange evacuated by road.	
—"—	6d		Visit Div. Train. Routine as usual.	
—"—	7d		Saddle rifle inspection. Visit by A.D.V.S. VIII Corps, I believe we are moving. Cpl. Lanfund very pleased with condition of stables & standings. Visit by D.A.D.V.S. 43d Div. & 33d Div. moves in to take over.	
—"—	8d		Wagons washed greased etc. then packed. Routine as usual.	

F.M.S.

WAR DIARY
or
INTELLIGENCE SUMMARY.

(Erase heading not required.)

Army Form C. 2118.

Instructions regarding War Diaries and Intelligence Summaries are contained in F. S. Regs., Part II. and the Staff Manual respectively. Title pages will be prepared in manuscript.

Place	Date	Hour	Summary of Events and Information	Remarks and references to Appendices
Sheet 28. S.29.a.2.4.	9th Oct.		Struck Camp moved to Sheet 28. M.16 a. 5.7 near WESTOUTRE. Arrived at 2.p.m. an open field, no covering. Any shed, we got some with later as some infantry transport moved out. Raining.	
Sheet 28 M16.a.57	10th		Went to 5 t. M.V.S. to see billet as we are taking over from them. Received orders to move to Sheet 28. M.6.a.2.7. tomorrow	
— " —	11th		Moved out at 10.a.m. arrived 12 mid day. I take over 23 animals 2/r. by 5 M.V.S. Visit by D.A.D.V.S.	
Sheet 28 M6.a.2.7	12th		Evacuated 26 animals to the Base by road. Sent 1 N.C.O + 2 men to C.M.D. X=Corps for duty. Draw 800 Francs for Pay of N.C.O.S + men. Gas appliance inspection.	
— " —	13th		No. 1/36629. Mr Tovey. Proceeds on leave to U.K. from 14th – 24th Destroyed 2 animals esp. by S. M.V.S.	
— " —	14th		Took over charge of 1st 2nd + 3rd Field Ambulances. Visited D.A.D.V.S. HQ. 7/AM. Treated on several animals. Wounded cases in great numbers coming in motor from hands	

WAR DIARY or INTELLIGENCE SUMMARY

Army Form C. 2118.

(Erase heading not required.)

Place	Date	Hour	Summary of Events and Information	Remarks and references to Appendices
Sheet 28 M.6.a.2.7.	14th		Continued. Wall of sand bags + earth erected around stables (D.R.S) as a precaution against bombs, raids in this area very frequent. Destroyed one animal. Saddle + rifle no friction.	
"	15th		Went to conference at Westoutre for D.A.D.V.S. who is ill in bed. Went to 43rd Field Ambulance afterwards at BOESCHEPE. Went 15 Div. H.Q. to arrange for dipping machine rugs. Destroyed 2 animals.	
"	16th		Visit H.Q. to see D.A.D.V.S. Went to ARAGON STABLES WESTOUTRE to down machine dip up for the Div.	
"	17th		A lot of horses and few men to deal with them everybody busy all day. Routine as usual.	
"	18th		Routine as usual.	
"	19th		Forwarded 21 animals to the Base by road. also 9 cases to C.M.D. and 10 tudes. Takes over duties of D.A.D.V.S. during his absence on leave.	F/WS

WAR DIARY or INTELLIGENCE SUMMARY

Army Form C. 2118.

Place: Sept 28. M.6.a.27.

Date	Hour	Summary of Events and Information	Remarks
20th		Visit 43rd Field Ambulance. Ref SE 4559. P.C. Lawson O. proceeds on leave to Scotland. from 21st to 31st	
21st		Visit by ADVS. 10th Corps. Operating all day on animals, pleas of horses coming in.	
22		Seventy mules horses in, crowded out. Visit H.Q. Received operating orders to move to Beveren. 24th inst. Lifting over from 7 Div. m.v.S. very heavy all day. BERTHEN. 24th inst.	
23		S/Sergt NOLAN. proceeds on leave (one month) 24/10/17 to 24/11/17. Evacuated 38 animals to the Base by dated 26 Sept. 17 3rd Anzac CCS. WIPPENHOEK. Destroyed one animal. Visit by ADVS road, 16 L5. my mules have been changed from Berthen to Boeschepe. Cap. 9.	O/c Records 2/3119/17
24		Reveille at 5.30 a.m. Landed over to 5th M.V.S. marched out at 11 a.m. arrived at 1 p.m. Lieut STEINER AVC reports for duty to relieve Capt O'CARROLL who is to take new command of this unit. I forwarded to Corps H.Q. to ADVS who was away, leaving a message asking him own 2 to forward	mt

WAR DIARY or INTELLIGENCE SUMMARY.

(Erase heading not required.)

Army Form C. 2118.

Place	Date	Hour	Summary of Events and Information	Remarks and references to Appendices
Sheet 27 R 4 a.7.2.	24th		Continued to No 2/3 V.H returned stating the fact I am acting DADVS.	
"	25th		Visit by ADVS X'th Corps, who gives me instructions. I am to apply for instructions to Div H.Q. I go to Div. H.Q. the A.A. & Q.M.G gives me definite instructions to proceed to the Base when I receive instructions from him as he wishes me to organise the clipping of the Div. I drive the machine from DADVS, went to ARAGON stables, got the men in, all equipment. I go to the 5th Div H.Q. to change oranything as per instruction NCO's & Corps Sanmal at ARAGON stables at 8.30.p.m. Horses one anxious in acquainting the needle etc so as to start work in the morning. I have one NCO there & one man with Section. Knife sharpener & two of the Corps. the machine. Coal oil, magneto amine as much as might. I report to Div. H.Q. progress.	
"	26th		Clipping going well, managed to clip 32 horses with 8 machines. Visit by DADVS M.G. I stay at clipping stables until evening. I go to Div'. HQ to report progress.	
"	27th		Capt O'CARROLL arrives at Section to take over command which I resume	

WAR DIARY
or
INTELLIGENCE SUMMARY

Army Form C. 2118.

Place	Date	Hour	Summary of Events and Information	Remarks and references to Appendices
Sheet 27 R.4.a.7.2	27th		orders to leave ARAGON Stables and start at METEREN. Just as everybody is going well have to start all over again. Got lorries report to move the lot. Send the horses away at once to new place, clear down clipping at 11 a.m. & went to Meteren to see to billets, stables etc. Someone for everything & visit H.Q. to report progress.	
"	28th		Went to METEREN. 40 horses clipped first day with 8 machines. Cpl AMOS AVC work very satisfactory, 3 new machines work very well. Report to H.Q. in the evening	
"	29th		No SE 4158 PTE HOBBS J. proceeds on leave to U.K. from 30/10 to 9/11/17. Visit Meteren clipping station, clipping running well, 40 done, 5 per machine. Visit Div. H.Q. & handed over equipment to visit to Capt O'Carroll RVC who was known O.C.	7/11/3
"	30th		Went to clipping station. Visit H.Q. Report progress	
"	31st		Went to clipping station. Report to AA+QMG & rank to be allowed to proceed to No 23 Division to start up the new Stations, expected that evening, to be in touch with them.	

Vol 30

<u>Confidential</u>

<u>War Diary.</u>

of

<u>O.C. 26th M.V.S.</u>

From Novr 1st to Novr 30th 1917.

(Volume No: 54)

Army Form C. 2118.

WAR DIARY
or
INTELLIGENCE SUMMARY.
(Erase heading not required.)

Instructions regarding War Diaries and Intelligence Summaries are contained in F. S. Regs., Part II. and the Staff Manual respectively. Title pages will be prepared in manuscript.

Place	Date	Hour	Summary of Events and Information	Remarks and references to Appendices
Sheet 27 R 4 a 7.2	1/11/17		Drawn 600 francs from Fd Cashier at ABEELE and paid NCOs & men of the unit. Routine as usual.	
	2/11/17		Evacuated 4 animals to the 10th C.M.V.D. and also 20 by road to No 23 Vet Hospital	
	3/11/17		Collected one ambulance case from 11th K. Limports at DICKEBUSCH and transferred it to the 10th C.M.V.D. at OUDERDOM.	
	4/11/17		Pte SE/21822 WEBB, G.W. AVC. Proceeds on leave to the united kingdom. Visited by the DADVS. Capt F.J. Weir leaves for No 23 Vet Hospital from the 5/11/17 — 10/11/17. Case from METEREN. Collected one ambulance	
	5/11/17		Went to Div HQ to interview the DADVS. Evacuated forty animals to No 23 Vet Hospital by road.	
	6/11/17		Evacuated 26 animals to the base by road. Routine as usual.	
	7/11/17		Washing waggons etc.: Visited by the DADVS.	
	8/11/17		Routine as usual; visited by ADVS. 10th Corps.; saddle kit inspection.	
	9/11/17		Visited by the DADVS. Went to Div H.Q. and received orders for the unit to entrain at BAILLEUL for WIZERNES on the 12th inst.	W. Carroll

WAR DIARY
or
INTELLIGENCE SUMMARY.

(Erase heading not required.)

Army Form C. 2118.

Place	Date	Hour	Summary of Events and Information	Remarks and references to Appendices
SHEET 27 R.44.7.2	10/11/17		Evacuated 12 animals to the 17 ANZAC M.V.D. Visited by D.A.D.V.S with whom I went by car to HODDSUTRE siding transport were remounts for the Division. Gas appliance inspection. One NCO & 2 M.en attached 4th, 1st & 2nd M.V.D retain to this unit further orders concerning the move received. to obtain arm at the 21st hour the Divisional clipping station to attached to this unit for the move. Routine as usual. I visited the Div Clipping Station at 14 eleven and saw that everything was thoroughly packed and ready to move the next day.	
	12/11/17		Evacuated 14 animals by road to No 23 vet Hospital St OMER. Packing/wagging to Strich Camp and moved off at 2.30 p.m. Arrived at 13 A.44.5.N.I.C. at 5 p.m. and into Arnid'. The train started at 9 p.m.	
WIZERNES.	13/11/17		Reached Wizernes at 3 a.m. detraining completed at 4 a.m. A place was allotted to me in a chalk quarry for my horse lines; not suitable in any way, however I got the horses fixed up there until daylight. At about 8 a.m I went with the D.A.D.V.S. in search of a better place for the horses and a got good stabling for all of them in a Chalk Factory. The horses are most comfortable. W.Carroll	
	14/11/17		Clipping of section horses begun and completed.	

A 5834 Wt. W 4973/M687 750,000 8/16 D. D. & L. Ltd. Forms/C.2118/13.

WAR DIARY or INTELLIGENCE SUMMARY.

Army Form C. 2118.

(Erase heading not required.)

Place	Date	Hour	Summary of Events and Information	Remarks and references to Appendices
Wizernes	15/11/17		Drew two francs from field Cashier St Omer. for pay of 1 NCO pmn. and also the clipping staff attached. Routine as usual.	
	16/11/17		Washing waggons etc. Routine as usual.	
	17/11/17		Evacuated 4 animals to No 2 B V et Hospital by road. Visited by D.A.D.V.S.	
	18/11/17		Saddle + rifle inspection	
	19/11/17		Evacuated 19 animals to No 23 Vet Hospital by road; riding of waggons etc. Our clipping station closed; men returned to their units	
	20/11/17		Went to Bosinghem + interviewed the A.V.C. Commandant about a mule left with an site abstract at West Becourt. + where pp... ceded and collected the animal and the inhabitant.	
	21/11/17		Received notification of SE/1232 Dr Barrow. W. was invaliated out of the area sick. No 21922 Dr Webb. G.W. returns from leave writing as usual.	
	22/11/17		No SE/3216 Sgt Roberts R L proceeds on leave from 23/11/17 to 7/12/17. Routine as usual.	
	23/11/17		Evacuated 7 animals to 23 V Hospital by road.	
	24/11/17		Gas appliance inspection. Routine as usual.	W Carroll

WAR DIARY
or
INTELLIGENCE SUMMARY.

Army Form C. 2118.

Place	Date	Hour	Summary of Events and Information	Remarks and references to Appendices
Wizernes	25/11/17		Marching order inspection: prizes given for best turn out: mounted & transport. The D.A.D.V.S. was present to judge. The turn out was really excellent	
	26/11/17		Routine as usual.	
	27/11/17		Drew 650 francs from the field cashier at ST. OMER for pay of NCOs men. Visited H. D.A.D.V.S.	
	28/11/17		Paid NCOs & men. Routine as usual	
	29/11/17		Collected a float case from No 4 Coy Div train at QUER CAMP. Routine as usual.	
	30/11/17		Evacuated 11 animals to No 23 Vet Hospital by road	

J. Carroll
Capt AVC

Confidential

War Diary

of

O.C. 26th M.V.S.

Decr. 1st to Decr. 31st 1917

(Volume No 55)

WAR DIARY
or
INTELLIGENCE SUMMARY.

(Erase heading not required.)

Army Form C. 2118.

Place	Date	Hour	Summary of Events and Information	Remarks and references to Appendices
Wijernes	1/12/17		Received orders to march to WINNEZEELE area on the 2/2/17. Route. Arques. Cassel. Starting point Arques at 2.12 PM. Billeting party to report at area Commandants office Winnezeele at noon on the 2/2/17.	
	2/2/17		Packing of waggons etc. Billeting party starts at 8 AM. and passed starting point up to time. The Section moved off at 12.30 PM. The march was very slow stoppages being frequent. Do. did not reach camp till 10 PM. At midnight I received orders to pass the starting point at Broxeelande at 7.30 AM, marching to Sheet 28. G 11 a 5.6.	
Sheet 28 G 11 a 5.6	3/12/17		Passed starting point up to time and reached camp at 12.30 PM. The camp had been left in a very dirty condition by the 15th M. the Veterinary Section	
	4/2/17		Cleaning up of camp etc.	
	5/2/17		Visited by D.A.D.V.S. routine as usual, received a number of sick animals, sent first to YPRES for mule belonging to 15/46 RFA	
	6/2/17		Saddle and rifle inspection. visited by A.D.V.S. VIII Corps. who informed me that guns in my lines area and must move. Later on in the day I received a message from the D.A.D.V.S. telling me that he was looking for a suitable billet for the Section. Admitted from sick animals.	
	7/2/17		Visited the D.A.D.V.S. No 601. Staff. Sgt Nolan returns from leave. Routine as usual. Admitted 7 sick animals.	

Army Form C. 2118.

Instructions regarding War Diaries and Intelligence Summaries are contained in F.S. Regs, Part II. and the Staff Manual respectively. Title pages will be prepared in manuscript.

WAR DIARY
or
INTELLIGENCE SUMMARY.
(Erase heading not required.)

Place	Date	Hour	Summary of Events and Information	Remarks and references to Appendices
Sheet 28 G 11 a.5.6.	8th		Routine as usual admitted 16 sick animals	
	9th		Gas appliance inspection. I sent for three ambulance cases belonging to D/45. Two of these were so bad that I had to destroy them on arrival. Evacuated 11 animals. Visited by Lieut Barham A.S.C. re shortage of rations. No SE 32/6 Sgt Roberts R.L returns from leave. Admitted four sick animals.	
	10th		SE 3518. Pte Squires J. AVC. reported for duty from No.2 Vet Hospital, in place of Pte Barnes invalided sick out of the area. Visited by the DADVS.; visited Div HQ. Sent for men but found that the F.O. Cashier had left. Collected one float ear. Pte PARTINGTON proceeds on leave from 11/12/17 to 24/12/17. Admitted 3 sick horses. One horse admitted from 8th Army 13th train with a mild N.F. had no shot in the N F or O H and on examination of the foot N F I found the sole very badly undermine, the course of least resistance forming an opening above the coronary band at the seat of quittor. No attempt seemingly had been made to deal with the latter condition and of course the pus following reports this matter to my DADVS today. In my short experience of a mobile Vet Section I find that in nearly all the cases of W to PUN OL (PUN) admitted at this unit there has not been a sufficient opening made for drainage; the Vet officer in charge should say has not dealt with the case himself but has left it in the hands of an inexperienced shoeing smith.	
	11th		Collected two ambulance cases from Ypres. Visited by the DADVS.	

W Carsrle

Army Form C. 2118.

WAR DIARY
or
INTELLIGENCE SUMMARY.

(Erase heading not required.)

Instructions regarding War Diaries and Intelligence Summaries are contained in F. S. Regs., Part II. and the Staff Manual respectively. Title pages will be prepared in manuscript.

Place	Date	Hour	Summary of Events and Information	Remarks and references to Appendices
SHEET 28 G.11 a 5.6	12/12/17		Routine as usual. Admitted 16 sick animals. Went to Poperinghe and drew 500 francs for pay of NCO's and men. Paid NCO's and men.	
	13/12/17		Evacuated 70 animals to No 13 Vet Hospital Neufchatel by rail from Ondurdom. Visited by DADVS. Pte Williams returns from Hospital	
	14/12/17		Routine as usual: visited by DADVS.	
	15/12/17		Saddle and rifle inspection received entire to-accuse my sick animals on the following day from Ondurdom at 11 am.	
	16/12/17		Inspected all my sick animals to Ondurdom but found that there was no train.	
	17/12/17		Visited by DADVS and ADVS.	
	18/12/17		Routine as usual collected two ambulance cases from Ypres.	
	19/12/17		Evacuated 32 animals to No 13 Vet Hospital Neufchatel by rail from Ondurdom. Visited by the ADVS and DADVS.	
	20/12/17		Routine as usual	
	21/12/17		Visited by DADVS.	
	22/12/17		Washing of waggons etc.	
	23/12/17		Went to Div HQ. routine as usual SE 8357. Pte Williams AVC proceed on leave from the 24/12/17 to 8/1/18.	

WAR DIARY
or
INTELLIGENCE SUMMARY.

Army Form C. 2118.

Place	Date	Hour	Summary of Events and Information	Remarks and references to Appendices
Sheet 28 G 11 a 5.6.	24/12/17		Evacuated 30 animals to 13 Vet Hospital via rail from Oudendom. Movement orders received to proceed to STOMER area on the 26th. Collected two ambulance doors.	
	25/12/17		Saddle and rifle and Gas appliance inspection. Loading of waggons etc	
	26/12/17		Struck camp and moved off at 9.30 AM. I sent billeting party off at 7.30 AM. to report to the area Commandant Zunnysulle by noon. The roads were very slippery, and so did not reach my billets before 10.30 PM.	
Wizernes	27/12/17.		Moved off at 10 AM. by STOMER to Wizernes which was reached at 5.30 PM.	
	28/12/17		Visited by D.A.D.V.S. Went to STOMER and drew money for pay of N.C.O's and men	
	29/12/17		Paid N.C.O's and men routine as usual.	
	30/12/17		Saddle and rifle inspection; billing of cookhouse etc. Movement orders received to move on the 31/1/18. by rail from STOMER to Eagehill.	
	31/12/17		Routine as usual.	

N. Campbell Capt A.V.C.
O.C. 26th M.V.S.

Vol 32

War Diary

of

O.C. 26 M.V.S.

January 1st to 31st

(Volume No. 56.)

WAR DIARY
or
INTELLIGENCE SUMMARY.

(Erase heading not required.)

Army Form C. 2118.

J Carroll
Capt A.V.C

Place	Date	Hour	Summary of Events and Information	Remarks and references to Appendices
Bray-sur-Somme	9/1/18	(continued)	Proceed to No 2 V.B.T. Hospital for transfer to Combatant units — No 35517 Pte Squires admitted to Hospital.	
"	10/1/18	—	Routine as usual. Gas Appliance inspection. Visited by D.A.D.V.S.	
"	11/1/18	—	Evacuated eight animals to the base by rail from Bray-sur-Somme. Visited by D.A.D.V.S.	
"	12/1/18	—	Routine as usual	
"	13/1/18	—	Saddle stuff inspection. Went to Div HQ and drew 600 francs for pay of NCO's and men	
"	14/1/18	—	Sent one Sgt, a Cpl and 9 men A.D.W. H.Q. to disinfect stable. Visited 43rd Infy Bde.	
"	15/1/18	—	Daily NCO's and men routine as usual.	
"	16/1/18	—	Evacuated 16 animals to the base from Bray sur Somme. Medical inspection of NCO's and Shoeing smith; tested all animals in the Section for Glanders. No 673 Sgt Card proceeds on the usual 14 days leave.	
"	17/1/18	—	Routine as usual. Visited by D.A.D.V.S.	
"	18/1/18	—	T.T. 025147. Pte Satchell proceeds on leave via Havre from 20-1-18 - 4-2-18. One Cpl and 2 men went to Div H.Q. to disinfect stable. Got 41st Infy Bde. Pte S Buckley, Harvey Thomson return from No 2 Vet Hospital being re-examined medically at the base they were classified B.	
"	19/1/18	—	Visited by Lt. A.D.V.S. & Lt. D.A.D.V.S. washing of waggons etc	

WAR DIARY
or
INTELLIGENCE SUMMARY

Army Form C. 2118.

26th MOBILE VETERINARY SECTION

Place	Date	Hour	Summary of Events and Information	Remarks and references to Appendices
Villers Bocage	1/1/18	—	Routine as usual.	
"	2/1/18	—	Harness cleaning and usual routine.	
"	3/1/18	—	Packing of waggons etc. Left Wiégenes at 5.30 P.M. for ST OMER where we entrained. Left ST OMER at 10.45 P.M.	
"	4/1/18	—	Arrived at Edge Hill at 8.30 A.M. and there had to wait for upwards of two hours before detraining was begun. Left Edge Hill at 11.30 A.M. and reached Bray-Sur-Somme at 2.30. Have had rain a very severe frost during the night so that the roads were very difficult for transport. DTs four horses on train.	
Bray Sur Somme	5/1/18	—	Routine as usual. Inspected the animals of the 4th F.E. Ambulance & the 89th F.E.	
"	6/1/18	—	Saddlery kit inspection. Visited the 47th & 49th Infy BDs. Visited by the D.A.D.V.S.	
"	7/1/18	—	Spared on the usual 14 days leave to Ireland.	W. Carmo Capt AVC
"	8/1/18	—	Command of the M.V. Sec. during my absence and Capt. Thomerville.	
"	9/1/18	—	Routine as usual.	
"	10/1/18	—	The following joined men No 526 Pte Hulls A; TT 02347 Pte Sinfield F; No 3500 Pte Boyden A.E; No 7583 Pte Bamber H; TT 02547 Pte H.K.A. North A.C. 2115/434 D.D. & V.E & I. Hd. North, N 816 2D.V.E & I. Hd. on their arrival; Pte S B 45 Rhys Harvey; Lou Smith, Y Small	

Army Form C. 2118.

WAR DIARY
or
INTELLIGENCE SUMMARY.
(Erase heading not required.)

Instructions regarding War Diaries and Intelligence Summaries are contained in F. S. Regs., Part II. and the Staff Manual respectively. Title pages will be prepared in manuscript.

26th MOBILE VETERINARY SECTION

Place	Date	Hour	Summary of Events and Information	Remarks and references to Appendices
Bray-Sur-Somme	20/1/18	—	Routine as usual. Visited by the D.A.D.V.S.	
"	21/1/18	—	Movement orders received: Collected 3 animals from Vrond - Sur Corbie and one mule from Bray-sur-Somme. Cpl Amos proceeds on leave from the 23/1/16 — 6/2/18.	
"	22/1/18	—	Evacuated 35 animals for base and 7 hulls. S.E. No 1050-2. D.T.E. arrive & proceeds on leave from the 26/1/18 — 9/2/18. The Section moved off from Bray Sur Somme at 9 A.M. and arrived at Rosaire en Santerre for the night.	
Rosaire en Santerre	23/1/16	—	Left Rosaire en Santerre at 9 A.M. and arrived at Damancourt at 3.30 P.M.	
Damancourt	24/1/18	—	Left Damancourt at 9 A.M. and reached Candor at 4 P.M.	
Candor	25/1/16	—	Left Candor at 12.15 P.M. and reached Tirlancourt at 4 P.M. Here I rejoined the Section from leave.	
Tirlancourt	26/1/18	—	H commo cleaning &c. Visited by D.A.D.V.S. : Sent some men along to Jussy to clear up & prepare new billet at Jussy.	
"	27/1/18	—	Sent some men along to Jussy to clean up & prepare new billet at Jussy.	
"	28/1/18	—	Left Tirlancourt at 11 A.M. and arrived our Jussy at 1 P.M. Sent along four men to disinfect stables for Div. H.Qrs. at Chauhi.	
Jussy	29/1/18	—	Sent our four men to Chauhi to complete the disinfection of stables. Visited by the D.A.D.S.	

W. Carroll
Capt. M.V.C.

WAR DIARY
or
INTELLIGENCE SUMMARY.

Army Form C. 2118.

Place	Date	Hour	Summary of Events and Information	Remarks and references to Appendices
USCy	29/1/18	—	SE/8500 DTE Baylis, A.E. transferred from this unit to No. 50 Coy M.V.S.	
			SE/4655 DTE Mitchell W.B. proceeds on leave to Scotland from 30/1/18 – 13/2/18.	
			No. 33 067 PTE E Bloomer H.C. reports for duty from No. 2 Vet Hospital in place of PTE Squire Cracroft. Received active horse into a new billet in jury.	
	30/1/18	—	Visited by D.A.D.V.S. "Disinfectng" of stables etc.	
	31/1/18	—	Visited by D.A.D.V.S. went over new billet and sent over a party of new transport, stable them. Drew 30 forage for pg of NCO and men. Saddle and rifle inspection and kit inspection.	

M. Cowie
Capt AVC
OC

Vol 34

Confidential

War Diary.

of

O.C. 26th M.V.S.

14 Division

February 1st to 28th.

(Volume No 57.)

WAR DIARY or INTELLIGENCE SUMMARY

Army Form C. 2118.

(Erase heading not required.)

Place	Date	Hour	Summary of Events and Information	Remarks and references to Appendices
Fussy	1/2/16	—	Routine as usual	
"	2/2/16	—	Packing of waggons etc. Visited by D.A.D.V.S.	
"	3/2/16	—	Moved into new billet in Fussy. Camp very dirty and very little accommodation for the men.	
"	4/2/16	—	Cleaning up of Camp. Visited by D.A.D.V.S.	
"	5/2/16	—	SE/7583 Pte Bromby W. and 33061 Pte Ellesmere proceded to No 2 Vet Hospital	
"	6/2/16	—	Routine as usual	
"	7/2/16	—	Visited by D.A.D.V.S. No 30252 Pte McLean proceeded	
"	8/2/16	—	Evacuated 40 animals to FORGES b.A.S.V.H. In charge of a party of 30 men. Arrived with all others in the Flay-limaret Area	
"	9/2/16	—	Visited by the D.A.V.S. and th. A.D.V.S. III Corps. who was so pleased with everything	
"	10/2/16	—	Saddle and rifle inspection and anti-gas appliance inspection. Received from A.S.C horses attached to the H.Q. 298 Bde R.F.A.	
"	11/2/16	—	Routine as usual. Visited by the D.D.V.S.	
"	12/2/16	—	Evacuated 10 animals to the base from Flay limaret some of the A.S.C horses attached to the 298 Bde H.Q. showed a doubtful reaction and cannot be sent with the others	
"	13/2/16	—	Routine as usual. Inspected the A.S.C horses att. 298 Bde H.Q. Much improvement since the day previous	McDowall Capt

WAR DIARY
or
INTELLIGENCE SUMMARY.
(Erase heading not required.)

Army Form C. 2118.

Instructions regarding War Diaries and Intelligence Summaries are contained in F. S. Regs., Part II. and the Staff Manual respectively. Title pages will be prepared in manuscript.

Place	Date	Hour	Summary of Events and Information	Remarks and references to Appendices
Juoy	13/2/18 (Cont)		Eye very much swollen, and forwards also, and a 7 from nasir Cantees and temperature 103°	
	14/2/18		Again inspected the ASC dental needles accompanied by the OTM/45. The usual careful discharge from mini Cantees and thermal reaction retained a positive reaction	
	15/2/18		Destroyed ASC AM 298 13909445 by order of ADVS Corps and on P.M. exam no lesion of glanders were found. Evacuated 4 animals to the base	
	16/2/18		Routine as usual began building a Cook House for the men	
	17/2/18		Visits by DADVS. Saddle and rifle inspection	
	18/2/18		Cook house completed; started on the building of a forge	
	19/2/18		Evacuated 12 animals to the base from Fleury le Martel	
	20/2/18		Routine as usual	
	21/2/18		Visits by DADVS	
	22/2/18		Evacuated 16 animals to the base and 3 hilo hinunealing of skin, etc	
	23/2/18		Took more dutin of ADVS during the usual temporary absence on leave	
	24/2/18		Receiving orders from ADVS to find a new site for the M.V.S. as to consider at present broken up for advance. Auspices appliance inspection	
	25/2/18		Spent most of the day trying to find new site for the M.V.S.	
	26/2/18		Evacuated 16 animals to the base	
	27/2/18		Routine as usual: washing from grey up.	
	28/2/18		Found a suitable place for the M.V.S. at Petit Valurie but am awaiting instructions from the ADVS before a moving	

Confidential

War Diary

of

O.C. 26 MVS

from April 1st to April 30th
1918.

(Volume No.   )

WAR DIARY
or
INTELLIGENCE SUMMARY.

(Erase heading not required.)

Army Form C. 2118.

Instructions regarding War Diaries and Intelligence Summaries are contained in F.S. Regs., Part II. and the Staff Manual respectively. Title pages will be prepared in manuscript.

Place	Date	Hour	Summary of Events and Information	Remarks and references to Appendices
BOURSINES	1/4/18		Moved at 11am. to COURMEILLERS.	
VERS.	2/4/18		Moved at 10 am. from Courmeillers to Vers. Drew money; and paid NCO's and men of the Section.	
Sheet Amiens 17. D2.	3/4/18		Moved at 10 a.m. to Sheet Amiens 17. D2. Spot where top line of letter E in Amiens crosses road.	
"	4/4/18		Major Blakeway Art. arrives and takes over the duties of OC AVS.	
"	5/4/18		Usual routine.	
"	6/4/18		Evacuated thirty animals to the base from SALEUX.	
"	7/4/18		REVEILLE at 3.30 a.m. Evacuated twenty four animals. Awaiting orders to leave to move the following day.	
"	8/4/18		Evacuated ten animals to the 4th Army V.C.S. at Picquigny. Packed up and moved off at 10.30 am. to FRESNOY au VAL.	
FRESNOY au VAL	9/4/18		Moved from FRESNOY au VAL to FRUCOURT.	
FRUCOURT	9/4/18		Moved from FRUCOURT to FEUQUIERES.	
FEUQUIÈRES	10/4/18		Routine as usual, entrained at Feuquières at midnight.	
	11/4/18			

WAR DIARY
or
INTELLIGENCE SUMMARY.

(Erase heading not required.)

Instructions regarding War Diaries and Intelligence Summaries are contained in F. S. Regs., Part II. and the Staff Manual respectively. Title pages will be prepared in manuscript.

Place	Date	Hour	Summary of Events and Information	Remarks and references to Appendices
PREURES	12/4/18	—	Detained at MARESQUEL at 9 am; and arrived at PREURES at 3 pm.	
"	13/4/18	—	Drew money for the pay of officers and men; Received warning orders to move to our Lille area.	
EQUIRRE	14/4/18	—	Moved from PREURES to EQUIRRE.	
"	15/4/18	—	Paid NCO's and men.	
"	16/4/18	—	Usual routine.	
"	17/4/18	—	Visits by visitors.	
"	18/4/18	—	Received orders to move to CAURON ST MARTIN on the following day and to establish an advanced post at MAZINGHEM.	
"	19/4/18	—	Evacuated thirty five animals to No 13 VET HOSPITAL from PERNES. Sent an NCO and four men to form an advanced post at Mazinghem. Although there were two Mobile VET. SECTIONS in that area, I moved off with the main Section at 3 pm to CAURON-ST-MARTIN.	
CAURON-ST-MARTIN.	20/4/18	—	Routine as usual.	

J. Carroll

Army Form C. 2118.

WAR DIARY
or
INTELLIGENCE SUMMARY.
(Erase heading not required.)

Instructions regarding War Diaries and Intelligence Summaries are contained in F.S. Regs., Part II. and the Staff Manual respectively. Title pages will be prepared in manuscript.

Place	Date	Hour	Summary of Events and Information	Remarks and references to Appendices
CAVRON-ST-MARTIN	21/4/18	—	Saddle and Rifle inspection	
"	22/4/18	—	Visited the D.A.D.V.S.	
"	23/4/18	—	Established another advanced post at DELETTE for the divisional artillery.	
"	24/4/18	—	Nothing to report	
"	25/4/18	—	Washing and oiling of wagons; order sues forth at HESDIN for the following day.	
"	26/4/18	—	Evacuated eighteen animals to the base from HESDIN; twelve to STOMER from the Advanced post at MAZINGHEM and thirty seven from the advance post at Delette. No 20946 Pte DRIVER A.M.Q.V.C. reports for duty from No 14 Vet Hospital	
"	27/4/18	—	Usual routine; a new float arrives to replace one destroyed by shell fire at JUSSY.	
"	28/4/18	—	Harness inspection	
"	29/4/18	—	Brought in my advance post from Delette	
"	30/4/18	—	Brought in my advance post from Mazingham	

JCCardle

Confidential

War Diary

of

O.C. 26th M.T.S.

from 1st to 31st May 1918

WAR DIARY
or
INTELLIGENCE SUMMARY

Army Form C. 2118.
25th MOBILE VETERINARY SECTION

Place	Date	Hour	Summary of Events and Information	Remarks and references to Appendices
CAVRON-ST-MARTIN	1/5/15		Unit of arrival in France 2/5/15 Went to Hesdin and drew 880 francs for pay of O.C. 6 & Men Paid N.C.O.s & Men typical orders received	
"	2/5/15		Convoi in eight animals to the Base from Helein. Stuck camp and moved off at 2 PM to Torcy via Sat-les-Hesdin. Visited by the D.A.V.S.	
TORCY	3/5/15		Continued as usual unshipf wagons etc. Visited by the D.D.V.S.	
"	4/5/15		Took over Veterinary Charge of 42nd Inf. Brigade	
"	5/5/15		Visited by the D.A.V.S.	
"	6/5/15		Routine as usual	
"	7/5/15		Visited 42nd Inf. Bde	
"	8/5/15		Received orders to proceed to Mt. 19th for Mult. Visits by the A.D.V.S. XI Corps	
"	9/5/15		Evacuated 17 animals to No. 23 Veterinary Hospital St. Omer (sent?) Visited by the D.A.V.S. Anti-gas appliance inspection	

WAR DIARY
or
INTELLIGENCE SUMMARY.

(Erase heading not required.)

Army Form C. 2118.

Place	Date	Hour	Summary of Events and Information	Remarks and references to Appendices
TORCY	10/5/18		Routine as usual. Capt E.S. Stenier A.V.C. took over command.	
	11/5/18		Capt O'Carroll A.V.C. left this unit for duty at No 19 Veterinary Hospital. 304 Pte Izzate transferred to No 19 Veterinary Hospital. Visit by the D.A.D.V.S.	
	12/5/18		Routine as usual. Kit inspection. Visit by D.A.D.V.S.	
	13/5/18		Saddle and Rifle inspection. Visited #2 Bde.	
	14/5/18		Went to Hadin to draw money for men for pay. 740 francs. Visit from D.A.D.V.S. Received orders to send 6 Privates to II Corps V.E.S.	
	15/5/18		Visited the 43 Bde. Paid men. Evacuated 7 Animals to No 14 Veterinary Hospital from Hadin.	
	16/5/18		Despatched 6 Privates to the II Corps V.E.S. Sgt 13433 Pte Cox E. A.V.C 20976 Pte Wynn A.H. A.V.C. 825 Pte Hicks C. R. A.V.C 4135 Pte Harvey T. A.V.C. 4593 Pte Jackson O.O. A.V.C 10502 Pte Cairns G. A.V.C 6 Rifles were taken. Visited #2 Bde.	
	17/5/18		Routine as usual. Visit from D.A.D.V.S.	E.S. Stenier Capt O.C

WAR DIARY or INTELLIGENCE SUMMARY

Army Form C. 2118.

Place	Date	Hour	Summary of Events and Information	Remarks and references to Appendices
Torcy	18/5/18		Mounted Inspection of Horses, Harness, Wagons and men. (Very Good).	
	19/5/18		Routine as usual. Visited 43 Bde. S6/4556 Pte Mitchell reports for duty from No 2 V.H.	
	20/5/18		Routine as usual. Cleaning wagons (oiling).	
	21/5/18		Visited by the A.D.V.S. XI Corps and D.A.D.V.S. and visited 42 and 43 Bde.	
	22/5/18		Capt Read M.R.C.V.S. A.V.C. reports to this unit.	

WAR DIARY or INTELLIGENCE SUMMARY

Army Form C. 2118.

Place	Date	Hour	Summary of Events and Information	Remarks and references to Appendices
TORCY	23/5/18		Capt. W.P.B. Beal A.V.C. takes over command of 26 M.V.S. from Capt. Steiner O.S.C. A.D.V.S. XI Corps & D.A.D.V.S. 14th Div visit 7th M.V.S. Brig. General & staff of 43rd Infantry Bde visit M.V.S. Sergt. Roberts A.V.C. during my absence called to see a cow that had recently calved. Cow down with nervous prostration after chipinel eating of first calf, gave 1½ grains strychnine. Cow gets up in about hours time	
	24/5/18		Routine as usual. Capt. Steiner A.V.C. leaves M.V.S. & returns to 14th Div. Train. Rifleman Kent. Cold shoes of 7th K.R.R. attached to M.V.S. for a refresher course of shoeing ordered. S.C. 26/5/23/5/18 Visited mens billets & cook house indented on C.A.D.O.S. overalls for cook. Handed in to DADOS 2 saddles.	
	25/5/18		There & 2 saddles unserviceable. Cow doing well. Officers on manual, DADVS. 14th Division visits M.V.S. Paid M.V.S. have no chaff cutter. Tried squeezing bale of hay with saw to chaff had it – very hard work & no better than axeing. Rifleman Lloyd injured right leg. Visited my outside unit 43rd Infantry Bde. Paquet reports one of our horses kicked out at a pleep seriously. Visited the men at billet & the men in fond & was asked when wounded front, found pack passing by & took its leg. Asked to leave & gave a prophecy of 2 days.	
	26/5/18		Sunday. Paid particular attention to forge foundry on shoeing work as usual at the expense of the cold shoes, told him Divo/dr the cold shoes to do as much as he could, & that Dr also wanted a alteration of the number of shoes put on daily sent into Wore. Friend cow doing well, regain no further attention. Saw sheep with broken leg. Shp/Att had put in splints, left well alone. About mentioned made fouled during day. 2 cobs sent in from 14th Div Hdqs as surplus. Forge statement 12 shoes put on made fouled during day. 2 cobs sent in from 14th Div Hdqs as surplus. Forge statement 12 shoes put on.	
	27/5/18		Routine as usual. Received 1 cob from 7 K.R.R./ an broken wind & ruined 1 cob. 7 K.R.R. B wider an incinerator Veterinary patients all doing well, great improvement in the 2 R.U.N. cases. Visited my outside Unit 43 Inf Bde Forge statement put on 10 shoes for outside units, 3 shoes for M.V.S. & 1 remove.	
	28/5/18		Visited rounds camp in a sanitary condition & all correct. Find field units standing in worry sing shoes, drew the staff Captain's 43 Inf Bde attention to this fact. Inspected V.F. equipment also to find signs of need or some of eunnists & informed the veterinary unit transp o. otherwise from base. Read secret document's map & made the necessary arrangements. Sergt. Roberts paints 1 wagon. Wrote to Area comat informing him outfit aerius & animals was to be had by applying to 26 M.V.S. Visited 43 2nd Inf. Bde units. Forge statement put on 10 shoes outside units & 2 M.V.S. Went to Hesdin 17 Kilos to draw 615 francs from Field Cashier total distance covered 34 Kilos on horseback. Paid men. Painting of wagons continued. Approved my stuff with ½ inch horse mask for inflicting hay seeds & flowers from hay. Forge statement put on 12 shoes outside units & 4 M.V.S.	
	29/5/18			

Costa
Capt. A.V.C.

WAR DIARY
INTELLIGENCE SUMMARY

Army Form C.-2118.

Place	Date	Hour	Summary of Events and Information	Remarks and references to Appendices
Torcy	30/9/15		Routine as usual. Harness Inspection. Replied D.C.O. 14th Divn Memo re Claim against M.V.S. Visited 12th Inf. Bde Civilian (french) patients doing well no further advice required. Letter replied to on date 29/9/15 to Area Comdt Royon. Posted up at Royon Forge Statement - 16 shoes put on for outside units.	
	3/10/15		Routine as usual. Patients of M.V.S. during week especially bad. Cases from 5/9 Division. M.V.S. visited by DADVS 14th Divn. Drew up Daily Routine orders M.V.S. sanded routine but defining the fatigues between 2.30 p.m - 4 p.m. Old salvage handed in to Ordnance. Visited units of 13rd Inf. Bde. Forge Statement - outside units 12 shoes. M.V.S. 7 shoes. Informed M.V.S. Cook to draw a menu up a post in Kitchen Cook House & hoped same into after at end of day. This is an excellent trait in M.V.S. are fed well.	

J.P.M.Deal Capt ac
O.C. 26 M.V.S.

WAR DIARY or INTELLIGENCE SUMMARY

Army Form C. 2118.

26 Mob Vety Sec[tion]
G.S. 37

Place	Date	Hour	Summary of Events and Information	Remarks and references to Appendices
Torcy			DATE of account in France 21/5/15.	
	1/6/15		Routine as usual. Wrote up diary for May month. Treated a post belonging to French Civilian at Licheyrs for broken knees. Read out on parade according to 1st Army Order two sentences for looting. Visited outside units of 42nd Div Arty. Forge statement.	
	2.6.15		Put up a brand for 26 M.V.S. Washing case civilian Torcy. Forge statement.	
	3.6.15	2:30 p.m.	Wazema. Calving case civilian Torcy. Forge statement. No 601 Staff Sergt. Nolan A.V.C. left the unit — for No 7 Vet. Hospital. Rifleman Lloyd left to join 33rd Division with Col Cullings Chargers. 2L.D. returned to run 67th Cav R.E. 2 Riders returned to run 42nd Cav R.E. Routine as usual. No 661 Staff Sergt. Nolan A.V.C. left the unit — for No 7 Vet. Hospital. Rifleman Lloyd left to join 33rd Division with Col Cullings Chargers. 2L.D. returned as one for Reemployment in the War Bond area. Took the wind of a Cleo. cob front & badly broken winded one not for Reemployment. Forge statement. Harness cleaning Baron required badly to have knuckles of harness cleaner. Forge statement. Routine as usual. Sick cab section horse Camp. Afternoon fatigue tidying up A.T.A. depot store. Visit G.O.A.D.V.S.	
	4/6/15		Sheep with swollen leg doing well. Forge statement.	
	5/6/15		Visited H.Q. 3rd Inf. Bde. had a case of mange in 7 K.R.R. Corps — 2 suspects, burnt brushes & all 3 animals, endorsed (burnt) painted 2 stables & saw to disinfection of them. Orlando lines Loots also sorted the sylve mentioned. Saddles. Lectured in stable management to training staff H.Q. 11th Kings Liverpool Regt. Officers very interested. After noon two of section drilled by Sergt Cood M.E. Forge statement.	
	6/6/15		Routine as usual. Demonstration to training staff of 11th Kings Liverpool Regt at R.V.S. Lameness & ageing. Saw Lt. Col Bingham D.S.O. made arrangements for 6 men to go through a Musketry course every afternoon from 2-4. p.m. Forge statement.	
	7/6/15		Demonstration to 11th Kings Liverpool Regt colors of horses; stable routine, a demonstration I thought would arrange the 2 cases being protests in R.V.S. After noon 6 men of M.V.S. shoot a Musketry course at the bar being of practising pte Bundy 20 points Cpl Sattfield 15 pts out of a possible 25 pts. I consider this good for men who have not shot since 1914. Forge statement.	
	8.6.15		Recruit as usual. Demonstration to 11th Kings Liverpool Regt continued. Officers show keenness in the course. Gave a short lecture on the anatomy of horse. Sergt Ream R.V.C. horse continues sick, continued hot kick. After noon NCOs & men continue their musketry courses. To-day 4 men gave 30 pts in grouping test. The Musketry instructor reports on men that it is very satisfied men show keenness & are improving. As I put up a prize for freshman & a prize for Sword class shots. Forge statement.	

A.P. Miles Capt AVC

WAR DIARY or INTELLIGENCE SUMMARY

Army Form C. 2118.

Place	Date	Hour	Summary of Events and Information	Remarks and references to Appendices
Tincy	9.6.18		Recd orders by D.R.L.S. from D.A.D.V.S. to move on 10th inst. to N17a7/3. Spent day in preparing & br, packing wagons & walking out billeting certificates. Recd 2 miles & re-issued the 2 miles to 6th Cavalry Reserve Park on authority of D.D.R. 1st Army, then continued their shooting course. Have met Programme of Move.	
DELETTE L'Olloir Wood N17a7/3	10.6.18 11.6.18	Left Tincy 9 a.m. arrived Delette 3:20 p.m. halting midday for 1½ hours. Left Delette 9 a.m. L'Olloir Wood about 1:15 p.m. Field Wood out & proceeded to pitched camp at Sheet "36 A N17a7/3. Then in turns in farm house near at hand, empty in dirt close to horse lines. Horse picketed to lines stretched between wagons present.	
	12.6.18		Routine as usual. Afternoon pickets putting up pickets horses. Received 3 tents authority Q per D.A.D.V.S. 14 Div. Received 3 lorries per Chinese Labour Group. Ammunition.	
	13.6.18		Routine as usual. Piloted 2 tents to Harness Room the other to Stores.	
	14.6.18		D.A.D.V.S. visits M.V.S. in morning. D.D.V.S. 1st Army togr. with A.D.V.S. XI Corps visits M.V.S. afternoon. Jenneroult.	
	15.6.18		4 lorries to XI V.E.S.	
	16.6.18		Telegram to report D.A.D.V.S. Office as soon as possible. I go there & hear staff of 14th Div. is leaving for England. Report myself again at Hdqrs 14th Division & learn X Corps instructions that I am to be the Actg. D.A.D.V.S. while Major Blakeney is in England. Routine in M.V.S. as usual.	
	17.6.18		Major Blakeney leaves for England. I take up duties as Actg D.A.D.V.S. & my other duties. From today the War Diary becomes a combined diary of M.V.S. & D.A.D.V.S. diary. Routine as usual. Visit XI Corps V.E.S.	
	18.6.18		Visit 14 Div Signals also visit 80 Labour Group to see a horse in Chinese Camp.	
	19.6.18		M.V.S. routine as usual. Put up identification board on lines. Visit 6 R.B. His mare attacked horse of 1st Army Auxiliary Co. A.V.C. with mange & evacuated to M.V.S. Evacuated Visit Q & ask to care to around units magnetic result. Float to learn to XI Corps V.E.S. galtions to M.V.S. 9 animals to Corps V.E.S.	
	20.6.18		M.V.S. routine as usual. Visit Transport of 5th Connaught Rangers. Rifle inspection & non-respirator drill. Visit 14 Div Train Hdqrs. accident, also labour return 2 animals with stern notion incident.	
	21.6.18		Spent morning in Office making out ack & 2330, ack & so on to visit Hdqrs X Corps again magnetic result. Afternoon fatigue in M.V.S. washing riding wagons. Visit 89 Field By R.E., also 63, 712, 725 Labour Companies.	
	22.6.18		M.V.S. routine as usual. Afternoon fatigue Cleaning harness & burnishing steel. Visit 61st Field Coy R.E., & also 159 & 733 Labour Companies. Received general animal return from 603 Division on the war 16th Division. Washed 1 horse Labrigin to puck evilian supping from mange at St Quentin.	

A.P.M.N
Captain

WAR DIARY
or
INTELLIGENCE SUMMARY.
(Erase heading not required.)

Instructions regarding War Diaries and Intelligence Summaries are contained in F.S. Regs., Part II. and the Staff Manual respectively. Title pages will be prepared in manuscript.

Army Form C. 2118.

Place	Date	Hour	Summary of Events and Information	Remarks and references to Appendices
L'Obscure Wood N17.A73	23/6/16		Routine as usual. Fatigue Washing & oiling Wagons. Visited N° 2 Coy A.S.C. & 5th Cameron Hr. Rangers.	
	24/6/16		Evacuated 7 animals to XI Corps V.E.S. Pte Impey & Williams report sick with P.U.O. "3 days fever".	
	25/6/16		Routine as usual. Visited N° 4 Coy A.S.C. 14th Div Train. 1 case ? mange evacuated to M.V.S. from 7.K.R.R.C. M.V.S. shoot. Ten Musketry Course on a Miniature Range 300 yards.	
			Maximum pts 25.	
			Sergt Card 23	
			Cpl Haynes 19	
			Pte Jones 17	
			Sergt Rohalet 16→ Cpl Fairfield 15	
			Pte Bradley 14	
			Pte Ashworth 14	
			Pte Mitchell 13	
			the remainder of men are 2nd Class shots.	
	26/6/16		Sent to DADOS 59 Divison 2 drew stores. Visited rounds. 62 Coy Field R.E. afternoon fatigue grazing	
	27/6/16		Evacuated 3 animals to XI Corps V.E.S. Routine as usual. Fasting water with 72 Sanitary Section.	
	28/6/16		Went to Rouquetoire drew money in payment of N.C.Os men. All animals out grazing during afternoon.	
	29/6/16		Routine as usual. Paid N.C.Os men. Received warning orders regarding move. Grazing whole	
	30/6/16		Sunday. Burnishing all steel work. Half holiday after noon.	

J M Bell Captain
O.C. 220 M.V.S.
Act D.A.D.V.S. 14th Div

1/7/16

Army Form C.2118.

WAR DIARY
or
INTELLIGENCE SUMMARY.
(Erase heading not required.)

Instructions regarding War Diaries and Intelligence Summaries are contained in F. S. Regs., Part II. and the Staff Manual respectively. Title pages will be prepared in manuscript.

Place	Date	Hour	Summary of Events and Information	Remarks and references to Appendices
OBLOIS Wood.	1/7/16		Routine as Usual. Evacuated 2 Animals to XI Corps Vet: Evacuating Station. Received Warning Order to move on 3rd inst.	
	2/7/16		Oiling & greasing all Wagons. Inspection of Harness. Also packing of Wagons.	
	3/7/16		Left Camp about 7.30 a.m. & arrived at Wisnes 3.15 p.m. Halted at Hurym outside Thérouanne. Then had Tea & sandwiches at midday halt.	
	4/7/16		Moved from Wisnes at 7.30 a.m. & arrived at Wierre Effroy about 4 p.m. This journey is a long & tedious one up & down hills, some of which are very steep. Great difficulty experienced by gun float Horses in keeping back float on steep hills & also in extending cradles. One horse had to float Horse in keeping back float, Halted at mid-day for 1½ hours. Horse watered & detailed noted nopes to keep back float. Halted at mid-day halt. Took Wedneway & R.D.V.S. 15th Divn returned jas. Then had tea & sandwiches at mid-day halt. Took Wedneway & R.D.V.S. 15th Divn returned jas. Then had tea & sandwiches at mid-day halt. & took over his duties. Present - 61 mo. apprentices as per return i.e. Hay knives up, knives, shingp. Routine as usual. Detailed fatigue to fix up Camp as per pattern i.e. Hay knives up, knives, shingp.	
	5/7/16		" " Camp in proper shape.	
	6/7/16		"	
	7/7/16		D.A.D.V.S. visits M.V.S. Wheel of P.A. Wagon shows signs of wood warping in Italian VP & places in wooden to set bones. After new fatigue all Wagons are washed. Visited Mb Cog Div Train Chiswell & horse 6 M.V.S.	
	8/7/16		Recd 1 horse from Nb Coy Div Train with Pneumonia, after exam: put pre all animals grey ist	
	9/7/16		Routine as usual. D.A.D.V.S. visits M.V.S. Two new yearlys all day passes to Boulogne as renewal of good work.	
	10/7/16		A.D.V.S. 7th Corps + D.A.D.V.S 12th Divn Inspects 26 M.V.S.. A.V.S. 7th Corps says Le is pleased with everything to soon the fort. A.D.V.S. 9 Lane emmunicated guns ministry into all punts such as stores, equipment, workhomes attorneys, billets of men musketry. After men fatigue dismissed & men given a half holiday as a reward of good work of appreciation of A.D.V.S. inspection. Received Warning Order to move on 12th inst.	
	11/7/16		Capt WRA BEAL AVC OTC 26 M.V.S. & also S.E. 76744 Cpl Haynes H.R. A.V.C. proceed on leave 7 absence to England from 11th 25 inst. - Evacuated 2 Animals to No 3 Vet Hosp.	Copies

WAR DIARY
or
INTELLIGENCE SUMMARY
(Erase heading not required.)

Army Form C. 2118.

Instructions regarding War Diaries and Intelligence Summaries are contained in F. S. Regs., Part II. and the Staff Manual respectively. Title pages will be prepared in manuscript.

Place	Date	Hour	Summary of Events and Information	Remarks and references to Appendices
CLERQUES	12.7.18		No. S.E. 4558 Pte Whitehall W.B.A.V.C. proceeds on special leave to U.K. 14 days. Struck camp & moved off at 6.30 am. Halted 1 hour at mid-day to water & feed. Arrived Clerques 5.30 p.m. Major Blakeway D.A.D.V.S. 14th Div. takes over command of M.V.S during absence of Capt. W. R. B. Deal O.C. 20 M.V.S.	
EPERLEQUES	13/7/18		Sgt. Clerques 12.45 p.m. & moved to Eperleques arrived there at 4. p.m. & pitched camp.	
	14/7/18		Cleaning up camp & making same as per pattern. Visited by D.A.D.V.S.	
	15/7/18		Routine as usual. Aftn: noon fatigue washing wagons	
	16/7/18		Routine as usual. Remainder built & painting different notice boards by Sgt. Roberts A.V.C. Aftn noon fatigue washing & cleaning harness	
	18/7/18		M.V.S. visited by D.A.D.V.S. who gave a lecture to different Transport Officers on Sammy D Inage 20 officers present. Parading of a Field Oven. 7h. V.S. visited by D.A.D.V.S. 7 officers	
	19/7/18		Routine as usual. Evacuated 5 animals to No. 23 V.H. M.V.S. visited by D.A.D.V.S.	
	20.7.18		G.O.C. 14th Division inspected 26 M.V.S. expressed his pleasure. Afternoon Half holiday.	
	21.7.18		Orders received from HQ whole G.S. green & whites while. Visited by D.A.D.V.S. Installed a rifle inspection. Received orders from Q. to wear animal sign on shoulder to be worn by all ranks of M.V.S.	
	22.7.18		Aftn noon fatigue Grazing of all horses. M.V.S visited by D.A.D.V.S. Sgt. Roberts takes over duties as clerk to D.A.D.V.S as his clerk went on special leave to U.K.	
	23/7/18		Evacuated 1 Mule & 1 mule to No 23 V.H. Routine as usual. M.V.S visited by D.A.D.V.S	
	24.7.18		Routine as usual. M V S visited by D.A.D.V.S	
	25.7.18		Capt. W.A.D. Seal A.V.C. & Corpl Haynes A.V.C. return from leave to U.K. Routine of M.V.S as usual. Capt. Deal takes over his duties as O.C. 20 M.V.S.	
	26.7.18		M.V.S. Routine as usual. Capt. W. R. D. Neal. takes over duties as acting A.A.D.V.S. Capt. D. Sent whilst imposed outside units S.A.A Carlton 14 D.A.C, 16th Manchester Regt & 14th Argyle & Sutherland Highland Regt.	
	27.7.18			
	28/7/18		M. V. S. afternoon fatigue cleaning harness.	

B. M. Deal
Capt R.V.C.

Army Form C. 2118.

WAR DIARY
or
INTELLIGENCE SUMMARY.
(Erase heading not required.)

Instructions regarding War Diaries and Intelligence Summaries are contained in F.S. Regs., Part II. and the Staff Manual respectively. Title pages will be prepared in manuscript.

Place	Date	Hour	Summary of Events and Information	Remarks and references to Appendices
EPERLECQUES.	29/7/18		Pte Mitchell W.B. A.V.C. returns from special leave to U.K. M.V.S. routine as usual. Visited the 12th Suffolk Regt in company with Sergt Romilly A.V.C. afternoon fatigue burning old paint & cart-eaulin & repainting wagon woodwork smartly	
	30.7.18		M.V.S. routine as usual. Inspected General Tempest's & Brigadier General Winser visit - M.V.S. visited May 14th Divisional Train & also Nos 2, 3, & 4 Companies of Train	
	31.7.18		Called to No 2 Coy of Div Train to stop bleeding in a horse kicked in hind fetlock in horse mastership annexe. M.V.S. routine as usual. 1 horse for course of lectures in horse mastership arrived.	

Jos M Reid Capt. A.V.C.
O.C. 26 B.V.S.

School of Horsemanship
at Mobile by Selim
(This & following pages)

WAR DIARY or INTELLIGENCE SUMMARY

Army Form C. 2118.

Place	Date	Hour	Summary of Events and Information	Remarks and references to Appendices
EPERLECQUES	1/8/18		Routine as usual in M.V.S. Evacuated 2 animals to 23 V.H. 1st Course Horse - mac. Griffiths commences at 26 M.V.S. 9 men attached for same report. Outside unit - inst. S.A.A. Lect. 14 D.A.C.	
	2/8/18		Painting Mess Cart for Divisional Horse Show. 1st Lecture to course	
	3.8.15		Routine as usual. Finishing Cart off. Harness & Stable Gear. Bot respirator drill	
	4/8/18		" " Rifle Inspection. Offs. men & inf. Holiday. Swimming & jumping Competitions 26 M.V.S.	
			Inst. By Maj. Jeans. 3rd prize middle & Lt. Francis J 20 Middle Rgt.	
	5.8.18		Inst. By Mac Jeans. Show a failure was numerous open events. Show well organised & well	
			Divisional Horse Show - Show attended & seen the D.E.T. 26 M.V.S. won 1st Prize in halt/single Horse won	
			was the best show I have attended & seen in the best stripped heavy draught Horse won	
			Turn out Mess Cart on Maltese Cart, 2nd prize in the show entering 5 entrants & winning three prizes	
			by Sgt. Tom. The 26 M.V.S. did well at this show entering 5 entrants & winning three prizes	
			the first time in the history that they have been placed as prize winners in Divisional Horse Show	
	6.8.16		M.V.S. Sent the [...] 14 M.T.Corps to be re-electro. D A D V S 4 Div visits	
			26 M.V.S & VIIth Corps visits 26 M.V.S. good work to O.C. NCOs & men	
	7.8.18		Routine as usual. Lecture to School of Trades & application. Cdl. Sheep J. XII Corps School Reproductions	
	8/8/18		M.V.S. visited by A.D.V.S. 14th Div. Sent in return to A.D.V.S. 4 Div showing M.V.S had treated 13 French	
			Civilian horses whilst stationed at Eperlecques. Rifle Insp. ITon Lecture to S. of H.M.	
	9.8.18		Routine as usual. Evacuated 3 animals to No 23 V.H.	
	10.8.18		Gas appliance inspection by Div Gas Officer. M.V.S. visited by A.D.V.S. 14th Div. Lecture to S. of H.M.	
	11/8/18		Animal evacuated to 23 V.H. A.D.V.S. VIIth Corps visits M.V.S. Routine as usual. Fatigue Harness cleaning	
	12.8.18		Capt Satchfield & Plt Mitchell proceed to No 4 V.H. for a course on Stewart-Clipping machine. Rifle	
	13.8.18		Inspection. Lecture to S. of H.M.	
	14.8.18		A.D.V.S. examine NCOs on School of Horse Mastership. 1 Bomb fell in a field 1000 yards	
			away. Mallein 55 horses of 9th Yorks Rances Rgt. Routine as usual	
	15.8.18		School [...] & men return to their units. Routine as usual	

WAR DIARY or INTELLIGENCE SUMMARY

Army Form C. 2118.

(Erase heading not required.)

Instructions regarding War Diaries and Intelligence Summaries are contained in F. S. Regs., Part II. and the Staff Manual respectively. Title pages will be prepared in manuscript.

Place	Date	Hour	Summary of Events and Information	Remarks and references to Appendices
EPERLECQUES	16/8/18		The 2nd Course of School of Horse-Shoeing assembles at 26 M.V.S. Routine as usual.	
	17.8.18		Evac: 5 animals to 23 V.H. A.D.V.S. VII Corps visits 26 M.V.S. Warning order Received to move into 2nd Corps Area. Proven. Routine normal.	
	18.8.18		Cold Shoer of VII Corps School returned to School. Packing up & Wagons oiling & greasing same	
Bisezelle	19.8.18		Fetched float from M.T.Coy. Lecture to S.of H.M.	
Strathcona	20.8.18		Struck Camp at 4 A.M. moved off at 6.15 a.m. arrived Bisezelle at 2 p.m.	
Sept 27	21.8.18		Set Bisezelle at 9.40 am & arrived at Strathcona Camp 2.35 p.m. Stables for bed. From Nivi & 6 Pros. Camp in dirty condition. First possibility of making camp smart & clean. Lecture to S. of H.M.	
F.3.Dr.9.	22.8.18		Tidying up Camp. N.wt. table 2 days to clean same. No S.E. 45.12 Pte Reikin w. proceeds on leave to U.K. from 22:8:18. – 5:9:18. Taken over 23 wire netting beds for men. Repairing Kitchen.	
	23/8/18		A.D.V.S. visits 26 M.V.S. Routine as usual. Build oven in Kitchen & cleaning up camp. Lecture to S. of H.M.	
	24.8.18		Routine as usual. A.D.V.S. 2nd Corps visits 26 M.V.S. Cutting long grass & weeding about stables. Tannery	
	25/8/18		Pub. Q. stables & lines. Sand bagging Meno Nissin Hut. Lecture to S.of H.M. Pte Bradly returns from Reinforcement details.	
	26.8.18		Routine as usual. Evacuate 5 animals to No.2. V.E.S. Digging drains around stables.	
	27/8/18		Routine as usual. Washing wagons & oiling same. Harness cleaning. Anti-fly drill quickest 7 secs average time 10 secs. Lecture to S. of H.M.	
	28/8/18		Evacuate 1 Mange case to 2 V.E.S. D.A.D.V.S. 14 Div. visits 26 M.V.S. Lecture to S. of H.M. Routine animal. Bracalett 2 animals & 2 mules	
	29/8/18		Routine as usual. Rifle Inspection. Rifle troubles & saddlery inspection	
	29.9.18		In bath to 2 V.E.S. also on loose hold. Lecture to S. of H.M.	
			Routine as usual. Evacuated 1 animal to 2 V.E.S. Lecture to S. of H.M.	
			Sgt Card & Pte Impey D this unit proceed on 14 days special leave to U.K. authority 2nd Corps. D.A.D.V.S. 14 Division visits M.V.S. & examines 9 men of School of Horse-Shoeing.	

WAR DIARY
or
INTELLIGENCE SUMMARY

Army Form C. 2118.

Instructions regarding War Diaries and Intelligence Summaries are contained in F.S. Regs., Part II. and the Staff Manual respectively. Title pages will be prepared in manuscript.

(Erase heading not required.)

Place	Date	Hour	Summary of Events and Information	Remarks and references to Appendices
Skotova Camp. Sheet - 27. F.13 Dl.9.	30/9/16		2nd Course of Lectures, School of Horse-Shoeing & h/ps terminates & men return to their units. Visit by ADVS 2nd Corps. Evacuated 6 animals to 2nd Corps V.E.S.	
	31/9/16		Routine as usual. Evacuated 6 animals to 2nd Corps V.E.S.	

[signature]
Capt. A.V.C.
O.C. 26 th M.V.S.
31/8/16

Confidential

War Diary

of

O.C. 26th M.V.S.

September 1st to 30th 1918

WAR DIARY
or
INTELLIGENCE SUMMARY.
(Erase heading not required.)

Army Form C. 2118.

Place	Date	Hour	Summary of Events and Information	Remarks and references to Appendices
Strathcona Camp Sub=27. F13 D1.9.	1/9/18		Routine as usual. Evacuated 5 animals to 2nd V.E.S.	
	2/9/18		Visited Field Cashier & drew 453/- francs for payment of men. Evacuated 13 animals to 2 V.E.S. Commenced laying bricks on stable floor.	
	3.9.16		Routine as usual. 3rd Course School Horse-mastership commences. O.A.D.V.S visits M.V.S.	
	4/9/16		Evacuated 4 animals to 2 V.E.S. Afternoon fatigues relaying stable floor with bricks.	
	5/9/18		Evacuated 3 animals, 1 Mule, to 2 V.E.S. Saddle & rifle inspection. Visited my outside units. Post Respirator inspection. Routine as usual. 3rd Lecture to S.g. N.C.M.	
	6.9.18.		Routine as usual. Drawing Camp, & continuation of flooring stables. O.A.D.V. visits to V.S. 2nd Lecture to S. g. N.C.M.	
	7.9.16		Evacuated 7 animals to 2 V.E.S. Rifle inspection including attached men. Afternoon fatigues relaying floor continued. 3rd Lecture to S.g. N.C.M.	
	8.9.18.		Routine as usual. Rain whole of day. Evacuated 5 animals to 2 V.E.S. 4th Lecture to S.g. N.C.M. D.A.D.V.S visits M.V.S. Commenced mining in camp. Report to R.1450. work undertaken in camp. Continuation of fatigues. Flood water drawn to Ardoine.	
	9/9/18.		Opening drain of camp after yesterdays flood. Routine as usual. Visit 5 stables. Visit 43 F.A. 4th Lecture to S. of N.C.M. Visit 12: F4g Sur Spds Visit 14: F.Amn Nos	
	10.9.18.		Routine as usual. Continuation of work on camp. 5th Lecture to S. g. N.C.M.	
	11.9.18.		2, 3 + 4 Corps.	
	12/9/18		Evacuated 4 animals to 2d Corps V.E.S. Lt. Tovey A.V.C. attached to 20 M.V.S. sentenced to 7 days C.B. for improper answer to an N.C.O. White washing camp inside cook house, latrine, & stables.	

A.M. Seal
Capt A.V.C.

WAR DIARY or INTELLIGENCE SUMMARY

Army Form C. 2118.

Place	Date	Hour	Summary of Events and Information	Remarks and references to Appendices
Skatawa Camp F.3. D1.9	13/9/18		Routine as usual. Evacuated 2 animals to 2nd V.E.S. Taking of roof & proto. 6" Lecture to School D.H.M.	
	14/9/18		Evacuated 12 animals to II V.E.S. Rifle Inspection. Visit H.3. F.A. DADVS visits M.V.S.	
	15.9.18.		Routine as usual. Butt rest picket inspection. Col Pick ands DSO visits M.V.S. Evacuated 3 animals to II V.E.S. Paid XCo's men.	
	16.9.18		Pte Partington A.V.C. leaves for II Army Rest camp Tilques to exchange a vicious mule. Examination of men & School of H.M. the men of this corner were notso good as the previous 67 men. Evacuated 3 animals to II V.E.S. Pte men of Sgt Hm return to their units. Visit of DADVS.	
	17.9.18		Warning order for movement.	
	18.9.18		Washing & greasing wagons wheels. Sent for float truck Moako not yet done.	
	19.9.18		Routine as usual. Evacuated 4 animals to II V.E.S.	
Hut 27, L23 d.4.9	20/9/18		Evacuated 2 Animals to II V.E.S.— Handed over Camp to 21 MVS 9th Div. We moved to Breda Farm horse Shelf 27, L23 d 4.9. Find ourselves in an old farm house RXI had been	
	21.9.18		Hay & found ranging camp. Routine as usual. Tidying up camp. Bulls humerous around salvage material collected. 2 Ponies are buttacked 26 M.V.S. to agree this company NDI By 14 Dir Fr S. Anderson acrg N° I Coy 14 2 Div Train transferred & attached to 26 M.V.S. DADVS visits M.Vs.	
	22.9.18		Return of Salvage material to Salvage dump. Saddle & rifle inspection.	
Hut 27 L23 d.4.9	23.9.16.		Routine as usual. One shell arrived in our neighbourhood about 300 yards away Killed 3 men wounded about 12 Officers men. Examination of another division on	

Jeff M Freel Capt

WAR DIARY
or
INTELLIGENCE SUMMARY.

Army Form C. 2118.

Place	Date	Hour	Summary of Events and Information	Remarks and references to Appendices
Breda Farm	24/9/18		ADVS XIX Corps visits 26 M.V.S.	
	25.9.18		Evacuated 10 animals to 7 Corps V.E.S.	
Rol'27. L23 d 4.9	26.9.18		B.E.J. & Colonel Wilson D.D.V.S. 2nd Army visit - M.V.S. D.A.D.V.S. visits M.V.S. General Moore D.V.S. Routine as usual. Went to view a site for advanced post at - H 32 a. find it surrounded by large guns of large calibre including a 15" howitzer & long range naval guns G.2. Satisfied post ground very bad pocked with shell holes.	
	27.9.18		Routine as usual. Evacuated 11 animals to VII V.E.S. + also 2 hides. Took over the duties of D.A.D.V.S. during his absence. Advanced post withdrawn to G29 b.5.5.	
	28/9/18		Visited advanced post- twice during day. slightly gassed (chlorine) in Reuthghilst. Patrolled found roads with PU mostly sidetrack to Hallebost Corner on look out for wounded animals.	
	29.9.18		Routine as usual evacuated 8 animals to No 7 V.E.S.	
	30.9.18		Routine as usual.	

Capt A.V.C.
O.C. 26 M.V.S.

Confidential

War Diary

of

O.C. 26th M.V.S.

1st to 31st October '18

WAR DIARY or INTELLIGENCE SUMMARY

Army Form C. 2118.

Place	Date	Hour	Summary of Events and Information	Remarks and references to Appendices
Breda Farm Sh.27.L.23.d.4.9	1/10/16		Routine as usual. Evacuated 7 animals to 7. V.E.S. A.D.V.S. XIX Corps visits 2.6 M.V.S. Visit Div. HQ. Recd Warning Order to move to Neuve Eglise. 	
	2.10.16		Evacuated 4 animals to 7.V.E.S. Moved off at 2.15 p.m. to Neuve Eglise and arrd at 4.45 p.m.	
Neuve Eglise Sh.28. T.14.d.2.8	3.10.16		Sited Camp on top of hill, roads in very bad cond. Found stables but them to pieces by shellfire. Standing can be made good. Visited by D.A.A.G. Afternoon petipue repairing standings & putting up rough shelter.	
	4/10/16		Genrl H.V. shells passed overhead into valley below camp. Routine as usual. Visited outside units 43rd F.A. 33rd L.A.M.Bty, 29 D 21. 16th V/L. Afternoon fatigues continuation	
	5.10.16		26 M.V.S. visited by Lt. Col. Perry A.D.V.S. XV Corps. Visited L. Amielot siding which is in its greenish muddle. & entrain horses to evac. Afternoon continuation of repairs	
	6.10.16		Routine as usual. Saddle, Bridle & box respirate inspection.	
	7/10/16		Evacuated 22 animals to XV Corps V.E.S at Strazelle. S.E. 4653. PUT Richmond proceeded on leave to U.K. from 8 – 22? Visited 41 F.A. & 61 Field Coy R.E. 29 D 21. Afternoon fatigues continuation repair of stables.	
	8/10/16		Paid NCO's men. visited 42nd F.A. Nailwel.	
	9/10/16		Routine as usual. Correspondence re shipping 14th Div.	
	10/10/16		Evacuated 9 animals to 15 V.E.S. Afternoon spent in dealing with back correspondence re A.D.V.S. actg white Major McLaunay on leave.	
	11/10/16		Routine as usual. Furnious air attacks for lorries during day. Clipped APM's horse & OC's horse.	
	12.10.16		Evacuated 6 animals to XV V.E.S.	
	13.10.16		Lt. Col. Mills A.D. XV Corps Horror activities in Mons A.D.V.G. in division self visited units. Inspection Anti-fire appliances.	
	14.10.16		Routine as usual. Saddle wipe Inspection. Went round with XV Corps Horror on the numerous visits of division.	
	15.10.16		P.A.D.V.S. 14th Division arrives from leave & absent.	
	16.10.16		Evacuated 10 animals to XV V.E.S.	
	17.10.16		D.A.D.V.S. 14th Div visits 2.6 M.V.S. Routine as usual. Afternoon camp fatigue.	
	18.10.16		Placed outpost at SH 27 P.32 C 4.4 Scherad Area opp Haynes settlement & Pte Jones. Rotary of Wagons. Evacuated 22 animals to XV V.E.S.	

J.P.M.

Army Form C. 2118.

WAR DIARY
or
INTELLIGENCE SUMMARY.
(Erase heading not required.)

Instructions regarding War Diaries and Intelligence Summaries are contained in F. S. Regs., Part II. and the Staff Manual respectively. Title pages will be prepared in manuscript.

Place	Date	Hour	Summary of Events and Information	Remarks and references to Appendices
Warwick Sud Hazebrouck Château	19/10/18		Moved off from Neuve Eglise 8:30 a.m. and at Papaard 11 a.m. mid-day halt water & feed. Arrived at Papaard 12:30 and Warwick Sud 3:30 p.m. rigged over portees & waggons. Float mackled war-burgh. Pontoon reported sound to Engineers who made bridge.	
	20.10.18		26.M.V.S. visited by AQMG & DADVS accompanied by DADVS 14th Div who gave us instructions to move next day to Tourcoing x 23.	
Ferme Montagne R. 29. X. 29. b. 2. 8. Tourcoing	21.10.18		Left Warwick Sud 8:30 and Ferme Montagne 2 p.m. Found Stables & billets.	
	22.10.18		Cleaning form up, disinfecting stalls, protect mangers. Afternoon cleaning billets. 26 M.V.S visited by DADVS 14th Div.	
	23.10.18		Duties as usual. Clipping & parading of 26 M.V.S. Remounting Evans ring made to see farmers. Visited by several inhabitants of Tourcoing. Visited outside limits No 2, 3, 4, Coy Div Train.	
	24.10.18		Routine as usual. Sold 2 horses to Aurelien for 500 francs each. Total 1000 francs, handed to 26 M.V.S. Visited by several Tradespeople who want to buy horses for work. G.S. Wagon made to Journeys cartying mangers on own billets & wool.	
	25.10.18		Routine as usual. Dorrupiate inspection. Afternoon jatique while washing proto-stables. Visited 43 2A Patrage group in Tourcoing meetings.	
	26/10/18		26 M.V.S visited by DADVS 14th Div. Visited Hg 14 DAC & No 3 Sect 14 DAC.	
	27/10/18		Routine as usual.	
	28/10/18		Saddlers 14 Div marks M.V.S. Saddles & rifles inspected.	
	29/10/18		Collected 1 German Horse from inhabitant at Antignies Tournai. Vet 7 inspects Thomas alteration visits 26 M.V.S. Sold 1 Horse to local butcher outside market 28 M.V.S expenses 500 francs. Col Perry ADVS XV Corps visits & inspects 26 M.V.S. expenses no approbation. The following orderlies proceed on leave abroad to U.K.	
			S.E. 30752 Pte the Stewart M. A.T.C S.E. 30746 S.S. Willett A. A.T.C T2/P46 S. Thomas E. A.T.C SE 51262 Pte Nolls J. A.T.C SE 41159 Pte Newson D. A.T.C	all via Calais
	30/10/18		Routine as usual. ODVS 14 Div visits 26 M.V.S. Jacoupy hires to inspect 14th DAC.	
	31/10/18		Evacuated to animals about 3 hides to 15th A.E.S.	

B.D. Bleal Capt a.v.C
O.C. 26 M.V.S.

Confidential

War Diary

of

O.C. 26 M.V.S.

1st to 30th November 1918

WAR DIARY or INTELLIGENCE SUMMARY

Army Form C. 2118.

Place	Date	Hour	Summary of Events and Information	Remarks and references to Appendices
Farm Montigue Sh. 26 N29 G.2.8. Tincourt	1/11/18		Routine as usual. Evacuated 3 Animals to 15th V.E.S. Visited 42nd L.H. at Herecourt.	
	2/11/18		After-noon fatigue running drill with rifles & machine gun.	
	3/11/18		Evacuated 14 animals to 15 V.E.S. Routine as usual. Inspected N° 1, 2, 3, 4, Corps 14th Div. Train. Trallened captured animals. 1 German Horse & 2 German donkeys.	
	4/11/16		26 M.V.S. visited by DADVS 14th Div. Town Major Tincourt visits 20 M.V.S. Routine as usual.	
Sh. 37. A 21 C.2.8. Wattelos	5/11/18		Orders to move to Wattelos packed up moved off at 11.30 a.m. and Wattelos 14.30.	
	6/11/18		Organising Camp, putting up tents to prepare, men billeted in empty House.	
	7/11/18		Routine as usual. 20 M.V.S visited by D.A.D.V.S. Visit held Cashier drew 500 frcs.	
	8/11/18		Washing wagons. Rate New men. New 1 School y woodfibre in issuing	
	9/11/18		Visited outside units N° 1, 2, 3, 4 Corps 14 Div Train. Box respirator inspection.	
	10/11/18		Evacuated 3 animals to 15 V.E.S. Rifle inspection. Cpl Salfield up to 15 rank Sephe hand.	
	11/11/18		Routine as usual. Saddle inspection. Visited outside units N° 1, 2 & 8 Res. 14th D.A.C. ARMISTICE Day. Information received that hostilities cease at 11 a.m. 10-day postal telegram on board. M.V.S. opened to see the first unit in the neighbourhood to receive curtailing. Telegram result being huge crowds assembled around notice boards, people cheer given crowd very feeling. Half holiday granted men. Signed out from return at 9 p.m. by order G.O.C. Division. Four animals evacuated to 15 V.E.S. Two captured donkeys sent to 15 V.E.S. for sale by DDR 2nd Army.	
	12/11/18		Routine as usual. Pte Webb W.G. proceeds on leave to U.K. 14.11.18 – 28.11.18	
	13/11/18		26 M.V.S. visited by DADVS 14th Div. 3 animals evacuated to 15 V.E.S.	
	14/11/18		Washing Wagons. Visited N° 1, 2, 3, 4, Corps 14th Div. Train.	
	15/11/18		Sergt Roberts proceeds on leave to U.K. 17.11.18 – 1.12.18. 7 animals evacuated to 15 V.E.S. Pte Wym Roydr. 1 load of Wood fibre for feeding.	
	16/11/18		Routine as usual. 13 animals evacuated to 15 V.E.S. Visited N° 1, 2, 3 Res 14 D.A.C.	

Army Form C. 2118.

WAR DIARY
or
INTELLIGENCE SUMMARY.
(Erase heading not required.)

Instructions regarding War Diaries and Intelligence Summaries are contained in F.S. Regs., Part II. and the Staff Manual respectively. Title pages will be prepared in manuscript.

Place	Date	Hour	Summary of Events and Information	Remarks and references to Appendices
Sh. 37 A.21. C.2.c Wattrelos.	17/11/18		Routine as usual. 12 animals evacuated to 15th V.E.S. 1 Animal collected from installant Mme Wyssen Neutcourt.	
	18.11.18		Lt. Col. Perry A.D.V.S. XV Corps visits 2 to M.V.S. Saddle & Rug Inspection. N2 Sect 16,OSO Parkington proceeds on leave to U.K. from 20.11.18 – 4.12.18. Routine as usual.	
	19.10.18		Animals evacuated to 15th V.E.S. Took over chicks from S.A.D.V.S. 14th Div who proceeds on Paris leave. No 83.57 Pte Williams proceeds on leave to U.K. 21.11.18 – 5.12.18. Routine as usual.	
	20/11/18		Evacuated 6 animals to 15th V.E.S. Visit-Bield Cookin drew 450 francs.	
	21/11/18		Routine as usual period NCOs men. Small Tables for mens room. Washing Wagon.	
	22/11/18		Visit A(4/7) + S(4/7) R.F.A.	
	23/11/18		Evacuated 4 Animals to 15th V.E.S. Visited outside units 42 F.A. Brew Ammo little	
	24/11/18		Inspection Saddles singles. Visited B/46, D/46 R.F.A.	
	25.11.18		Routine as usual. Visited No 3 Coy Agst. 14 Div Train & No 1 Sect 14 DAC.	
	26.11.18		Visited 4.2nd Inf Adv, 6th Welsh, 14 A.M.S.H. 10th Pembroke Regt. Leave to U.K. from 28.11.18 – 12.12.18. Evacuated 6 animals to 15 V.E.S.	
	27.11.18		No 7871 Pte Jones proceeds on leave to U.K. from 28.11.18 – 12.12.18.	
	28/11/18		Evacuated 3 Animals to 15 V.E.S. Routine as usual. Clearing tidying up Camp. Circular re breeding mares. Visited B/46, B/46, No 1 Sect 14 D.A.C. picked out horses.	
	29.11.18		Evacuated 3 animals to 15th V.E.S. Visited S.A.D.V.S. Office afternoon. Routine as usual.	
	30.11.18		Box inspection inspection. Washing 3 Mens changes. Routine as usual.	

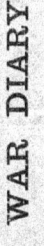

Emmel
Capt. A.V.C.
O.C. 26 M.V.S.

Confidential

War Diary

of

O.6. 26 M.V.S

(From 1st to 31st Decr, 1918.)

Army Form C. 2118.

WAR DIARY
or
INTELLIGENCE SUMMARY.
(Erase heading not required.)

Place	Date	Hour	Summary of Events and Information	Remarks and references to Appendices
WATTRELOS Sheet 3Y A21.C.2.8.	1/12/18		Routine as usual. Inspection of Rifles & Saddles	
	2		Inspection of Wagons & general routine	
	3		Sgt Roberts AVC returns from Leave	
	4		Routine as usual. Corpl Salkeld AVC proceeds on leave to UK 5/6 19/12/18	
	5		Visited Units	
	6		Visited 39t. HQ. Pte Partington AVC returns from Fever	
	7		A course of Colin Stewering held at 26 MVS. Visited Div HQ. Major Blakeway's RAVC (DADVS 14" Div) death reported	
	8		2 Animals to No 15" VES	
			Visited Div HQ. Routine as usual. Sgt Roberts admitted to F. Amb.	
	9		Visited ADVS X Corps. 4 Animals to No 15" VES	
	10		Visited Div HQ. Routine as usual. 3 Animals to 15-" VES	
	11		Visited Div HQ. 1 Animal to 15-" VES	
	12		Visited Div HQ. 1 Animal to 15-" VES	
	13		Inspection of Mules from units of 14" Div by DDRCAD VS X Corps 6 DADVS 36 Div. 18 mules were selected transfer to mounted troops from 124 mules forwarded for inspection. The horses were very pleased with the condition of the animals	
	14		Visited Div HQ. 3 Animals to 15-" VES. No 7341 Pte Jns TR returns from leave CyrillaP?BRown	

Army Form C. 2118.

WAR DIARY
or
INTELLIGENCE SUMMARY.

(Erase heading not required.)

Place	Date	Hour	Summary of Events and Information	Remarks and references to Appendices
IN ATTRELOS	1918 Dec 15		Visited Dn HQ. Routine as usual.	
Shut 3Y	16		Sandells Rifle inspection. Visited Dn HQ. Capt P.R. Lumn RAMC arrives.	
A2Y C/2.4	17		Inspection of 26 MVS.	
			Visited by A.D.V.S. 15th Corps. Visited Dn HQ	
	18		Visited Lieut Anchie XV Corps. Draw 960 francs for pay of NCO's + men	
			Capt P R Lumn RAMC takes over command of 26 MVS from Capt WP Bryant	
			RAMC who becomes a/DADVS 14th Dn.	
			Visited No 3 Co. In Dn Train	
	19		Routine as usual. Paid NCO's + men	
	20		Visited 42nd Inf Bde.	
	21		1 animal to 15th VES. Cpl Sackett RAMC returns from leave in UK	
	22		3 animals to 15th VES. Section photographed. a/DADVS being present.	
	23		1 animal to 15 VES. Routine as usual. Visited 3 Co in Dn Train	
Shut 3Y	24		3 animals to 15th VES. Move 25/17 VS 6 Artillery Shut 3Y. A2Y A5Y.	
A2Y A15.Y			Pte Johnson 1072 proceeds on leave to UK. Period 24/12/18 to 9/11/19	
	25		Arrive at ROUBAIX mk No 1 Co in Dn Train. Capt Bond RAMC present.	
	26		Visited No 1 & 3 Co 14 Dn Train. No 21832 Pte Webb returns from military	
			Hospital NORTHAMPTON.	

APLumn
Captain

Army Form C. 2118.

WAR DIARY
or
INTELLIGENCE SUMMARY.
(Erase heading not required.)

Instructions regarding War Diaries and Intelligence Summaries are contained in F. S. Regs., Part II. and the Staff Manual respectively. Title pages will be prepared in manuscript.

Place	Date	Hour	Summary of Events and Information	Remarks and references to Appendices
Roubaix Sheet 3Y A24A5-7	1918 Dec 27 28 29 30 31		Routine as usual. 7 Animals to 15" VES Visited #2 Inf. mob. Veterinary Routine as usual. Walker to train. Changed men billets 10 Animals to 15" VES Routine as normal.	

MMDmore
Capt. R.A.V.C.
26-11-15

<u>Confidential</u>

War Diary

of.

O.C. 26th M.V.S.

(January 1st to 31st 1919)

WAR DIARY or INTELLIGENCE SUMMARY

Army Form C. 2118.

Place	Date	Hour	Summary of Events and Information	Remarks and references to Appendices
WATTRELOS Sheet 2y A 24. A.5.y	1.1.19		Routine as usual. Drew forage 440 from Cachus XY Corps Spare NCO's men	
	2.1.19		Visited 42 Infantry Div Transport	
	3.1.19		18 Animals received from No 6 of 74 DAC. 4 Animals evacuated to 15 VFS	
	4.1.19		14 more Animals evacuated to 15 VFS. The Vet mine here Mr Allyluto	
	5.1.19		Sample Rifle Inspection	
	6.1.19		Veterinary Board for Categorizing Animals commenced at No 1 Sec 67FR 1H. DAC Amended Veterinary Board at No 2 & 3 Sec DAC. 10 Animals evacuated to 15 VFS	
	7.1.19		To complete animals of 14 DAC. Visited by DADVS 13 Animals evacuated to 15 VFS	
	8.1.19		" 2/46 " B/46 Bde RFA	
	9.1.19		" C/46 & D/46 "	
	10.1.19		" "	
	11.1.19		" "	
	12.1.19		To complete animals of H6 Bde RFA 5 Animals to 15 VFS	
			" 96 Bde RFA. Visited by DADVS. Rifle Swulle	
	13.1.19		at 96 RFA. 8 Animals evacuated to 15 VFS Inspection	
	14.1.19		No SE 24282 Pte Fanthorp W. RAVC reports from No 2 Vet Hospital for duty with the unit on duty from R.F.A HQ & 16 3 Co 141 Bn 1min at D/46 RFA & No 2 Co 14 Bn 1man. Drew fce from Cachus XV Corps. No 643 Sgt Curie R RAVC Proceeded on Special farm to UK Period 16·1·19 to 30·1·19	
	15.1.19			
	16.1.19		Routine as usual. Paint NCO's man	
	17.1.19		No SE 24 282 Pte Fanthorp W. RM VC Proceeds to No 2 Vet Hospital in accordance with instruments received from RAVC Records Base. Amended Vet Mount. 61, 62 Jt ONE PARK	

WAR DIARY or INTELLIGENCE SUMMARY

Army Form C. 2118.

Place	Date	Hour	Summary of Events and Information	Remarks and references to Appendices
WATTRELOS Sheet 5I A 24 A 5. 7	18.1.19		Visited No 8 Co train. 7 Animals of 15 VES. Sent in stores rejected by Remount Depot.	
	19.1.19		Mullened animals of 42 Inf. Bde Transport.	
	20.1.19		Mullened remaining animals of 42° Inf Bde Transport also No1 Co 14 Don Train.	
	21.1.19		Mullening No 7 Co train & 26 DVS.	
	22.1.19		Routine as usual.	
	23.1.19		Visited by DADVS.	
	24.1.19		Routine as usual.	
	25.1.19		7 Animals evacuated to 15 VES. 3 Animals sold to Abattoir WATTRELOS. Visited by DADVS.	
	26.1.19		Routine as usual.	
	27.1.19		Went with DADVS to mallein 61 Fd Co RE. No 659 Sng/King J. QARC reports for duty from No 1 Vety Hospital.	
	28.1.19		Malled 61 Fields RE.	
	29.1.19		Destroyed 3 Animals at Abattoir Wattrelos. Mullened 62 Fd Co RE.	
	30.1.19		Visited 62 Fd Co RE	
	31.1.19		Visited 14 Div HQ. Evacuated 8 animals to 15 VES.	

P.P. Plumer
Capt RAVC
O i/c 26.VS.19

Confidential

War Diary

of

O.C. 26 M.V.S.

(1st to 28th February 1919.)

Army Form C. 2118.

WAR DIARY
or
INTELLIGENCE SUMMARY.
(Erase heading not required.)

Instructions regarding War Diaries and Intelligence Summaries are contained in F. S. Regs., Part II. and the Staff Manual respectively. Title pages will be prepared in manuscript.

[Stamp: 6TH MOBILE VETERINARY SECTION]

Place	Date	Hour	Summary of Events and Information	Remarks and references to Appendices
Rombai	1.2.19		No STE 30/44 S/S Mitchell A. RAVC proceeds to UK for demobilisation	
	2.2.19		Notification received that No 1012 Pte Johnson J.R.RAVC has otherwise Released	
	3.2.19		Evacuated 5 Animals to 15 V.E.S.	
	4.2.19		" " " 15 V.E.S.	
	5.2.19		" "D" Animals to 8 V.E.S. Mules - 1 + 3 Expo train	
			" " " "	
	6.2.19		H6 M & RFA C in DAC	
			Visited XV Corps Centre to pay in money attorneys for Demarnal	
	7.2.19		Visited DHQ to take over from DADVS who proceeds on Workways leave	
	8.2.19		" " " " " Section visited by DDVS & Army ADVS XV Corps	
	9.2.19		Visited DHQ	
	10.2.19		" " Drew 500 francs from pay-master. Received new horses	
			20 M V & R 15 VES (transit in sale of 2 animals	
	11.2.19		Visited DHQ	
	12.2.19		Visited DHQ also 46 R.E.T.C. 14 DAC. Move 9 26 7VS & 15 VES	
			(26 Pontoon and Industrial) completely isolated No 693 Sergt R	
Touring	13.2.19		Cmd RAVC return from leave	
			Visited DHQ	
	14.2.19		DHQ	

D. D. & L., London, E.C. (A700) Wt. W1 71/M291 750,000 5/17 Sch. 52 Forms/C2118/14

Army Form C. 2118.

WAR DIARY
or
INTELLIGENCE SUMMARY.
(Erase heading not required.)

Place	Date	Hour	Summary of Events and Information	Remarks and references to Appendices
Tournai	15.2.19		Visited DHQ. 46 RFA 16 DAC 1 & 3 Coys 14 Trans	
	16.2.19		" DHQ	
	17.2.19		" DHQ	
	18.2.19		Visited DHQ on D ammunt. butcher & water Journey	
	9.2.19		Visited DHQ	
	20.2.19		" DHQ & Field Cashier to Pair in 767 50 fr D Anneau	
	21.2.19		" DHQ DADVS return from leave	
	22.2.19		" DADVS	
	23.2.19		Visited Field Cashier & V Corps —	
	24.2.19		Me Z Annual Returns from 20 MVS & 7 DVS. total.	
	25.2.19		Visited DHQ & Field Cashier.	
	26.2.19		" Drew 526 francs for ordy from AVH.	
	27.2.19		No. T/T 03913 St Archer J. AVC reports for ordy from AVH.	
	28.2.19		Visited by DDVS V Army.